Letters
from
the Front

Letters from the Front

BOYS TOWN ON THE BATTLEFIELD FROM PEARL HARBOR TO THE PERSIAN GULF

by

Terry L. Hyland and Hugh J. Reilly

Foreword by U.S. Sen. Bob Kerrey

BOYS TOWN, NEBRASKA

Letters from the Front

Published by The Boys Town Press
Father Flanagan's Boys' Home
Boys Town, Nebraska 68010

Publisher's Cataloging in Publication

(Prepared by Quality Books Inc.)

Hyland, Terry.
  Letters from the front: Boys Town on the battlefield from Pearl Harbor to the Persian Gulf / Terry L. Hyland and Hugh J. Reilly.
    p. cm.
  Includes bibliographical references and index.
  ISBN 0-938510-51-7

  1. Father Flanagan's Boys' Home – Biography. 2. Soldiers – United States – Correspondence. 3. United States – Armed forces – Military life – History – 20th century. 4. Father Flanagan's Boys' Home – History.   I. Reilly, Hugh J.   II. Father Flanagan's Boys' Home.
III. Title.

HV876.H95 1995   362.7'4'09782254
                                  QBI95-20057

★　★　★

*This book is dedicated to these former Boys Town citizens
known to have given their lives in our nation's wars.*

World War II

Jack Bailey
Charles W. Brazda
Duane Brown
James Burns
William Capps
Edward Carr
James Conroy
Vernon Crowley
William Debbs
Franklin Dennick
Anton Druskis
George H. French
Thomas Gapa
Robert E. Gough
Dale Grafe
Robert Grant
Richard Haidusek
Marvin Harding
Charles Holman
James Keane
John C. Le Count
Charles Magnusson

Joseph Marino
Robert E. McCarthy
Patrick K. McKenna
Donald Monroe
David H. Newberry
William Parnell
Martin Peluch
Arthur C. Pfeifer
Maynard Reiner
Louis Rewitzer
Gerald E. Selleng
Paul Solt
Earl Tharp
George A. Thompson
Clarence Vainreb
Raymond Vorce
Robert Wiskochil
Charles E. Wood

Korean War

Gene Paul Blake
Thomas J. Blataric
Myron L. Cutler

John Gonzales
Arnold Lederer Jr.
James R. Shepard

Vietnam War

Robert Cordova
Douglas Frederick
Louis M. Garcia
Guiseppe Giannelli
George A. Hain
Raymond Hanik
Billie Frank Hewitt
Leonard Hultquist
Joseph F. Keeney
Robert E. Lutz Jr.
Nathaniel Murphy
Frederick H. Newman
Steven Noggle
James Sampers
John K. Schmitt
Forrest Stafford
Wesley Tomaszewski

★ ★ ★

Table of contents

★　★　★

Foreword
By U.S. Sen. Bob Kerrey

Letters from the Front, through gripping, heroic, often implausible tales, paints a picture that is the goodness of the human spirit.

It poignantly illustrates the power of family, of hope, of faith, told through the eyes of individuals who by all rights deserved to be familiar with none of those traits.

It tells us stories of young men struggling to survive humankind's greatest failures — war, brutality, the destruction of lives and of families. The common bond which allowed these men to overcome the struggle was their understanding of what it meant to love, of what it meant to belong, of what it meant to be a part of a family. Yet, ironically, the stories told in *Letters from the Front* are told through the eyes of men who, as a consequence of life's starkness, its harshness, its inconsistencies, had every excuse not to know the beauty of belonging or the love of family.

It is this irony that makes *Letters from the Front* so powerful. For at its most fundamental level, *Letters from the Front* tells the story of Boys Town.

It was Boys Town which offered hope to lost souls who had previously been introduced only to hopelessness.

It was Boys Town which substituted love to young men for whom life previously had seemed a bitter journey down a lonely and desperate road.

It was Boys Town that gave boys discipline and provided understanding. It was Boys Town that became family.

And ultimately, as these pages so powerfully illustrate, it was Boys Town that gave these young men the values, the fortitude and the courage needed to persevere.

Letters from the Front is an important addition to the body of literature which helps us understand who we are and what we can become.

Bob Kerrey, a native of Nebraska and a highly decorated Vietnam veteran, is a former member of the elite Navy Sea, Air and Land (SEAL) Team, the Navy version of the Green Berets. In 1970, President Richard Nixon presented Kerrey with America's highest military award, the Congressional Medal of Honor for Kerrey's "conspicuous gallantry and intrepidity at the risk of his life above and beyond the call of duty." Kerrey, who was severely wounded in the war and lost his right leg below the knee in battle, is the only current member of Congress to have received this award. Kerrey was further honored when the United States Navy renamed the SEAL Team I training camp in Southern California, Camp J. Robert Kerrey.

★ ★ ★

Introduction

Stay with me, God. The night is dark.
The night is cold: my little spark
Of courage dies. The night is long;
Be with me, God, and make me strong.

A Soldier — His Prayer

As sailors, they braved the perils of the open sea; as airmen, they took the fight to the enemy high above the earth; as soldiers, they battled their way through steamy jungles, over scorching desert sands, and across muddy fields. They served in different branches of the service, and fought in different times and places. They all called Boys Town their home.

Since Boys Town was founded in 1917 as a haven for orphaned, abandoned, and troubled boys, more than 2,000 of its former residents have served in the armed forces. At least 63 are known to have died in combat, and scores more have been wounded.

1

This book honors the wartime contributions of Boys Town and its residents. From Pearl Harbor, where three boys were killed in the attack that drew the United States into World War II, to the return of our victorious troops from the Persian Gulf in 1991, it chronicles the battlefield experiences of many of those whose lives were touched by Boys Town.

Their stories are about the courage of Boys Town's heroes, the sacrifice of those who died or were wounded, the bravery of those who faced torture and deprivation as prisoners of war, and the perseverance of those who quietly did their duty and came home. Not forgotten are the events and efforts on Boys Town's home front, from war bond and scrap metal drives during World War II to a massive campaign to send letters to every Boys Town citizen serving overseas during the Persian Gulf War.

The sources tapped to bring this book to life include interviews graciously given by Boys Town veterans, newspaper clippings and magazine articles, historical records, books, and photographs from the Boys Town Hall of History archives. And there are the letters — the all-important link to home — written by Boys Town "kids" from the battlefields of World War II, Korea, Vietnam, and the Persian Gulf. In their own powerful words, this is where they shared their fears, their longing for home and loved ones, and their hopes for peace.

Boys Town is proud of its war veterans and all of its former residents — men and women — who have served in the military. They hold a special place of honor at the Home, where children have found healing and hope for more than 75 years.

In 1991, Boys Town dedicated a memorial to its former residents who served in the armed forces. Inscribed on the memorial are these words from President John F. Kennedy's 1961 inaugural address:

"Ask not what your country can do for you; ask what you can do for your country."

Like the memorial, this book is dedicated to those who embodied that ideal of service and sacrifice.

World War II

The radio announcer had barely finished reporting the shocking news that Japanese planes had attacked Pearl Harbor when the entire population of Boys Town showed up at Father Edward Flanagan's doorstep.

It was December 7, 1941, a chilly winter day in Nebraska. Christmas was less than three weeks away, and Boys Town had started preparations for the holiday season. But now a time of joy was overshadowed by the realization that America was going to war.

Led by the mayor, the boys crowded around Father Flanagan, beseeching him to let them enlist in the service. The priest could see that all of them, even the youngest, understood that their country needed them.

Father Flanagan was proud of his boys. They had lived through some hard times, before and after coming to Boys Town. Most were children of the Great Depression, and almost every one had known hunger or loneliness or the feeling that no one cared. Boys Town had given them a second chance, teaching them to take pride in themselves and in their country.

During the months that followed the United States's entry into the war, hundreds of Boys Town "kids" lined up at the enlistment stations. Some of the older boys were allowed to enlist immediately, and the entire Class of 1942 joined up after graduation. Many former Boys Town residents went into the service, too.

On the home front, Father Flanagan was named chaplain of "America's War Dads." Later, when hundreds of former Boys Town residents were in uniform, he would be proclaimed "Number One War Dad in America."

Father Flanagan watched his boys go off to war with pride and sadness. He was like a father to most of them, and like any concerned parent, it was hard to see your children leave. So many boys had lived at the Home over the years, but all of them were special to the tall Irish priest who still called even his oldest charges "Dear."

On the battlefields, the young men of Boys Town served honorably and bravely. They were at Pearl Harbor, Guadalcanal, Bataan, Normandy, and hundreds of other places whose names will be remembered only by those who were there. Many were cited for bravery under fire. At least 40 were killed in action, and hundreds more were wounded.

Boys Town contributed to the war on the home front, too. The boys collected tons of scrap metal and iron, rubber, and anything else that could be used in the war effort. They planted Victory Gardens, growing acres of vegetables and grain crops on the farm. They listened to the radio for war news every chance they got, and read about the exploits of America's fighting forces in magazines and newspapers.

Father Flanagan, sometimes accompanied by Boys Town veterans, toured the country to speak at war bond rallies. During a one-week tour in November 1942, Father Flanagan sold nearly $3 million in war bonds. War bonds were on sale at Boys Town, too.

Father Flanagan also stayed in touch with his boys overseas. He wrote hundreds of letters to former Boys Town residents during the war, and received hundreds of letters in return. When a serviceman needed a lift at the front, he could always count on

Father Flanagan or someone from Boys Town to come through with a letter.

As the war went on, so did Boys Town's work. Orphans, kids from broken homes, and young men with no place to turn made their way to the "City of Little Men." The Home had become very well-known after the release of the popular 1938 movie, *Boys Town*, starring Spencer Tracy and Mickey Rooney, and the Home's population had swelled.

That meant Father Flanagan had to make plans for a bigger, better Boys Town. He envisioned a postwar expansion that would double Boys Town's size and put up new cottages, schools, and administrative buildings all over the campus.

All through the war, Father Flanagan's thoughts were with his boys, those who were in harm's way and those who might soon be there. Each time a boy came home safely, there was a joyous homecoming. Each time a telegram arrived notifying him that another boy had fallen, there was grief and sadness.

In late 1945, after the war had ended, the City of Baltimore presented Father Flanagan with a blue flag. Sewn onto the flag were two stars — on one was an "800," the number of Boys Town citizens who were known to have served in the armed forces during the war. On the other, a gold star, was a "35," the number of men who were known to have died in combat. (The final number of combat dead would be 40.)

The flag would be a constant reminder of the war's terrible toll. But it also served as a testament to the sacrifice and courage of the Boys Town residents who had given their all.

Father Flanagan knew his boys would never give anything less.

A place called Pearl Harbor

They were all Father Flanagan's boys. Orphans and refugees from the road.

Donald Monroe was born in Webster Groves, Missouri. William Debbs and George Thompson were from Omaha, Nebraska, and Walter C. Clark was born in Ashland, Ohio. Their lives first entwined at Boys Town in the 1930s. On December 7, 1941, in a place called Pearl Harbor, they shared a moment in history.

William Debbs was the first of the quartet to arrive at Boys Town. Abandoned by his mother, he and his siblings were placed in St. James Orphanage when their father died. William was 13 when he came to Boys Town in September of 1932.

It took some time for him to adjust to his new life. He struggled with Latin, arithmetic, and homesickness. In June of 1933, he ran away from Boys Town to see his brothers and sisters in St.

James Orphanage. He returned to Boys Town the next day and promised Father Flanagan this time he would stay.

He stayed through the drought of that summer when he and the other boys formed bucket brigades to save the vegetable gardens. And he stayed through the winter that brought deep snows and freezing cold. He was here in March of 1934 when George Thompson first came to Boys Town.

George Thompson's mother told Father Flanagan she had no fuel in her house to keep her son warm nor food to keep him fed. The ravages of the Great Depression had forced many families to turn to Boys Town to care for their sons.

When George Thompson came to Boys Town, it was still a very small place. The boys lived together 24 hours a day, so it's certain that George and William knew each other. They may have fished together or played marbles. William may have even lent George some of his precious detective and western magazines. In the end, George stayed four months. Just long enough for his mother to get back on her feet again.

George's stay made a lasting impression. In a letter to Father Flanagan, he wrote, "I will never forget Boys Town or the friends I made there." Many he would never see again, but he and William Debbs were destined to meet once more.

William thought of Boys Town as home now. William had settled into a routine at Boys Town: school, working on the farm, and band practice. He played the trumpet in the band and developed a lifelong love of music. He was an old hand by the time Donald Monroe and his brother came to Boys Town in the autumn of 1935.

Donald Monroe's father had died of pneumonia in 1935. His mother had died several years earlier. In July of 1935, Julia Hynes of the St. Louis Department of Public Safety, first wrote to Father Flanagan to tell him about ". . . two wonderfully good boys. Both their mother and father are dead. They are fifteen and fourteen years of age." Miss Hynes asked Father Flanagan to give the boys "the training they need to fit them for bigger and better things in life."

Father Flanagan wrote back, saying Boys Town "would gladly accept Donald and his brother." They arrived at Boys Town on September 16, 1935.

Donald Monroe had never been away from home and Boys Town must have seemed a strange and exciting place. His love for music prompted him to join the band and it was there that he first got to know William Debbs. Members of the band toured small towns near Omaha through that winter and spring. The boys raised money for the Home through their concerts and kept up with their studies while they were on the road.

Father Flanagan wrote to Miss Hynes in St. Louis that:

> . . . The boys have behaved themselves
> rather well for the time they have been with
> us, especially Donald. He has been a very
> exemplary figure and a source of edification
> to the other boys here at the home. All in all,
> he is a perfect gentleman and we are very
> proud to have had him with us.

In July of 1936, Donald and Ralph Monroe went back to St. Louis to live with their aunt. However, a short stay at Boys Town was often a long and meaningful time in the life of a troubled boy. Donald left his mark on Boys Town and the Home left its mark on him. He enlisted in the Navy in 1939.

William Debbs had no family to take him back. His family was Boys Town and when his younger brothers joined him there in the autumn of 1936, his family was complete. William left Boys Town in the spring of 1937. Father Flanagan had found work for him on a farm near Cresco, Iowa. He continued to play his trumpet and was a popular figure at the dances in the area. In April of 1940, he wrote Father Flanagan that he was going to join the Navy. Like his friends Donald and George, he was continuing a Boys Town tradition of service to his country.

And like his friends, he would be missed. Shortly after join-ing the Navy, William received a letter from a girlfriend of his in Iowa. She wrote: "I'm glad you like the Navy because you find so many boys who don't. Those are the ones who never worked when they were at home and didn't have to obey anybody. But you've gone among people to make your own living. I bet you like the dances and the girls out there. I think quite a few girls miss you out here, no lying either."

The last of the quartet was just arriving at Boys Town around the time George Thompson and Donald Monroe enlist-ed. Walter C. Clark, an orphan, was a "pilgrim" who came walk-ing in off the road in the autumn of 1939.

His mother had died when he was 18 months old. His father cared for Walter and his two brothers and four sisters for five years after their mother's death. Then he lost his job. The children were placed in the Children's Home in Ashland, Ohio, when Walter was 5. Walter's father died of heart problems the next year. Walter was the youngest in his family and was cared for by an older sister when he left the Children's Home. When her husband lost his job during the Great Depression, Walter was on his own again. He drifted into work with the Civilian Conservation Corps in Utah and stayed there until some boys threatened him with a knife.

Like many boys on the road, Walter had heard about this place called Boys Town. A place where a boy like him would be safe, with food in his stomach and a roof over his head. He hitch-hiked east from Utah and wound up on Father Flanagan's doorstep in October of 1939.

When Walter arrived at Boys Town, more than 200 boys lived there. Ken Maynard, star of western movies, had just visit-ed, the football team had won its 35th straight game and before the year was out, Boys Town would be featured in the popular comic strip "Joe Palooka."

Walter's time at Boys Town had a strong impact. Even after

he left to try and join the Navy he turned to Father Flanagan for help. Because he was absent without leave from the Civilian Conservation Corps, he had difficulty joining the military. However, through the influence of Father Flanagan, Walter was able to get his record cleaned up and he joined the Navy that summer. Now the paths of all four boys began to merge.

In August of 1940, William Debbs wrote Father Flanagan: ". . . I am here at Great Lakes Naval Training Center and I like the Navy just fine. I appreciate all you have done in helping me get into the Navy. I will never regret joining the Navy."

Debbs was shipped out to Hawaii, where he was stationed on the USS Oklahoma. While on the ship, he met an old friend, shipmate George Thompson. The two reminisced about their time at Boys Town and laughed at what a small world it really was. Father Flanagan received a letter from Walter Clark in October of 1940.

> I'm thankful for everything that was done for me at Boys Town. How's the football team coming along this year? I hope they can continue their winning streak.
> Our ship, the USS West Virginia, will soon join the fleet on the west coast. I could never seem to get used to sleeping in those hammocks but I finally got used to it. They are eight feet from the deck and if you ever fall out of them you really know it. On my leave I'd like to come back and visit Boys Town if I can. I wish I knew some of the boys' names so I could write to them. I forget all the names. Well, I just wanted to let you know I'm still thinking of you. Just one of your boys,
>
> Walter C. Clark

In January of 1941, William Debbs wrote home to Father Flanagan from Pearl Harbor, Hawaii. While the war raged in Europe, it was quiet in his part of the Pacific.

> This is a swell place out here.
> Everything is so green and there are lots of
> flowers.
>   Our ship is one of the oldest ones in the
> U.S. Fleet. It has fought in the World War. It
> went on a goodwill tour around the world in
> 1938. I would have liked to have been in the
> Navy that year. This sure is a swell life for a
> young man as he gets to see a lot of the
> world and learn more every day. May God
> bless you.

The fourth member of the quartet soon joined his friends in
Hawaii. The letter Donald Monroe wrote to Father Flanagan
arrived in July of 1941.

> I am now in Honolulu. It's very warm
> here. I saw the (motion) picture on Boys
> Town. We had it on our ship the USS Arizona.
> It was wonderful! I enjoyed myself. Everyone
> enjoyed it. All the boys on my ship ask me
> was Boys Town just like in the picture? I told
> them it was. They also ask me were your
> ways just like in the picture? I told them that
> was you up and down.

That same July the Boys Town Band participated in a con-
cert at Soldier Field in Chicago to celebrate "Americanism Day."

Father Flanagan gave a speech asking for support for
Franklin D. Roosevelt's defense program: ". . . The chief executive of our nation has issued a call to our people and the peoples
of the democracies of the Western Hemisphere to establish a
defense program in order that we, who love our liberty and our
American way of life, may be prepared to defend our rights
against any marauding powers. We have taken up that challenge.
We could do nothing else. . . ."

In less than five months, four of Father Flanagan's boys
would be taking up that challenge in a very personal way. Their
part of the Pacific was about to erupt in war.

On October 22, 1941, George Thompson wrote to his uncle's family from the USS *Oklahoma*.

> Howdy Folks:
>   . . . I never felt better in my life. The only thing wrong is that it is pretty hot out here around the islands. We have been out to sea since Friday morning and it will be another week before we get back to Pearl Harbor.
>   I like it fine aboard ship, sure is a good bunch of fellows and they feed me swell. I don't know for sure when we will get back to the States again. We're supposed to go to drydock in Bremerton for a couple of months in April. It might be longer though now that the Japs are giving us something to think about; I hope not.
>   Well I guess I had better quit as I think it's about time to 'darken ship' and they turn the lights out here in the library, as it's on the main deck.

Thompson was right about the Japanese. They gave the servicemen at Pearl Harbor "something to think about" just over a month after he wrote his letter.

December 7, 1941, dawned cool and crisp at Boys Town. The local movie houses in Omaha were playing *Sergeant York* starring Gary Cooper, and *Buck Privates* with Abbott and Costello.

In the Pacific, it was just another Sunday morning for Donald Monroe. He was a long way from his home at Boys Town. He awoke at his usual time and began preparing breakfast for his shipmates on the *Arizona*.

The bombs began to fall shortly before 8 a.m.

There had been rumors and warnings of an impending Japanese attack but they had been discounted as unlikely. Even as the first Japanese planes appeared over the islands, many people watching thought it was just another training flight gone awry. It was the bomb explosions and the smoke and the flames that changed their minds.

Admiral Kimmel, commander in chief of the U.S. Pacific Fleet, watched as the first wave of Japanese planes swept into Pearl Harbor. "I knew right away that something terrible was going on, that this was not a casual raid by just a few stray planes. The sky was full of the enemy." He saw "the *Arizona* lift out of the water, then sink back down — way down." Admiral Kimmel was later court-martialed for spacing the ships and planes too close together, making them easy targets for Japanese bombs.

Donald Monroe probably never heard the bombs fall. It was all over so quickly for him and hundreds of his shipmates. John Crawford, Chief Boilermaker on the *USS Vestal*, anchored alongside the *Arizona*, watched as a torpedo swept underneath his ship and "blew the bottom out of the *Arizona*."

On the deck of the *West Virginia*, Walter Clark watched as the Japanese planes flew overhead. In a letter to Father Flanagan, he recalled that horrible day.

> The seventh of December was a peaceful morning. The sun was just coming over the mountains. And at 7:50 a.m. death and destruction came out of the sky. Lots of the fellows were still sleeping, others working and still others getting ready to go to church. We were taken by surprise. But it didn't take long to man our battle stations. General Quarters was sounded, but by that time, we had been hit several times by heavy bombs. The ship caught fire and started blowing up. Other ships in the harbor were also hit by this time. The gun I was on didn't get many rounds out. But instead I helped fight fires and care for the wounded. I had several close friends killed and I sure hated that. But most everybody lost friends there.

The killing blow for the *Arizona* came from a bomb that struck beside the Number Two turret and exploded in the forward magazine. It was probably the explosion that Admiral Kimmel witnessed from the shore. Its force tore the ship apart and scattered bodies and debris on all the adjacent ships. Walter Clark's shipmate, Marine Fiske from the *West Virginia*, remembered seeing the *Arizona* blow up. "She just rained sailors," he said.

Almost 1,000 men died when that bomb hit, including the highest ranking officers aboard the *Arizona*, Admiral Kidd and Captain Van Valkenburg. Ultimately the *Arizona* was hit by eight bombs in addition to the hits from torpedoes.

Fourteen hundred men slept aboard the *Arizona* on December 6. Fewer than 200 survived the next day's attack. The rest are sleeping there still. Donald Monroe sleeps with them.

As the *Arizona* sank to the bottom of the harbor, William Debbs and George Thompson were fighting for their lives on the *Oklahoma*. The call, "Man your battle stations! This is no drill," alerted Debbs and Thompson to their danger. By the time they grabbed their equipment, two torpedoes had already ripped into the *Oklahoma*.

The ship was hit a third time and began to list noticeably. It was clear to the experienced sailors aboard that the *Oklahoma* was going to capsize. The ship's executive officer, Commander J.L. Kenilworthy, gave the order to abandon ship and men climbed and jumped overboard as the *Oklahoma* began its slow death roll.

Some men were perched along the spine of the ship when the fourth torpedo hit. The *Oklahoma's* bosun, Adolph M. Bothne, said that when it exploded, "the ship seemed to hesitate. Then, she bounced up, and when she settled down she turned over." Several of the men slipped and scrambled down into the water.

There were men trapped inside the capsized hulk who

weren't freed until the next day when rescuers, following faint taps from the desperate men pounding on the inside hull of the ship, cut them out. Electrician's Mate 1st Class, Irvin H. Thesman, said of his rescue: "It was a deep powerful feeling, like being dug out of your own grave."

George Thompson and William Debbs never made it safely off the ship and into the water. They may have been killed when the Japanese torpedoes slammed into the ship or by the fires and explosions that followed. They may have survived inside the capsized hulk for a time, trying to make someone hear their frantic hammering.

Did they think about their home thousands of miles away, or was it over too quickly for them to think at all? If they survived those first few horrifying minutes, was it a comfort to know that their friends were with them at the end? Did they fear no one would remember them?

They were not forgotten.

Father Flanagan wrote George Thompson's mother of the loss — and the pride — that he felt in her son's sacrifice.

> It is with a heart full of sorrow that I write extending to you my sincere sympathy in the death of your son, George, but at the same time I extend to you my heartiest congratulations — because of the pride that must be in your heart today for having brought into the world a son who paid the supreme sacrifice for his country.
>
> It is mothers like you, dear Mrs. Thompson, who are the real patriots of our country and we all admire that patriotism and that courage — and we are buoyed up with still greater enthusiasm to carry on in order that our Country may continue to enjoy the freedoms which the blood of our forefathers made possible for us.

George Thompson was Boys Town's first confirmed casualty of World War II. He would not be the last. In April of 1942, Father Flanagan received a letter from the Navy concerning Donald Monroe.

> . . . Since the Japanese attack on Pearl
> Harbor December 7, 1941, Donald Monroe
> has been carried on all our lists as 'missing
> in action.' I believe that the Navy Department
> will soon declare all men still missing in this
> category as a result of the above attack
> 'dead.'
>
> I knew Donald Monroe very well as he
> was attached to my mess. He was a fine
> example of what a young American should
> be, and in every sense more than lived up to
> the very highest standards set by our Navy
> and our country.
>
> Donald Monroe was proud of Boys Town;
> I know that Boys Town is proud of him. If he
> was an example of the average boy from
> Boys Town, then I can easily see why our
> whole country is proud of Boys Town.

Walter C. Clark was the only one of the four Boys Town boys to survive the attack on Pearl Harbor. But he did not survive the war unscathed. In September of 1943, he wrote Father Flanagan from a hospital bed in Charleston, South Carolina.

> I sure was happy the other day when I
> received the Boys Town Times in the hospital
> here. I'm waiting for a medical discharge
> from the Navy. My nerves went bad on me
> due to all the battles I've been in. I was in
> Pearl Harbor during the sneak attack and my
> ship was sunk in the harbor.
>
> Then I went on the USS Lexington and
> was with it when it was sunk in the battle of
> the Coral Sea a year ago. Later I went aboard
> the USS Edsall and had several narrow

escapes. When I'm discharged from the Navy
I hope to land a job at Douglas Air Craft
Factory in Los Angeles. Please write me soon.
I would love to hear from you. Just one of
your boys,

                                         Walter

Walter got his medical discharge. The youngest of the four
Boys Town boys at Pearl Harbor, he had the chance to grow
older. He moved to California, got married, and raised a family
of his own.

Many others at Pearl Harbor were not as lucky. More than
2,300 American servicemen died on that fateful Sunday morning that forever changed America.

William Debbs was 22; Donald Monroe was 21, and George
Thompson was only 20 when they were killed. They were all just
boys. And they will remain boys forever.

Just one of your boys, Father. Just one of your boys.

Peril in the South Pacific

August of 1931 was a terrible month for Billy Capps.

His mother died, and his father abandoned him. Only 15, he was left in the care of his grandmother, Mrs. Mary Shores.

"I am old and unable to do much work," Mrs. Shores wrote Father Flanagan. "Billy is ambitious and of a very fine disposition. He is willing and mild and anxious to make the best of his possibilities." Father Flanagan wrote back to Mrs. Shores that, "Billy is welcome at Boys Town."

Billy left his home in Ogden, Kansas, and arrived at Boys Town just after Father Flanagan left on a six-month leave of absence. Never a healthy man, Father Flanagan was sent away to rest and recuperate from the daily pressures of running his home for boys.

Billy arrived during a perilous time for Boys Town. Father Flanagan was in a Denver hospital and financial problems were

threatening the Home's existence. In an appeal for help in
September of 1931 Father Flanagan wrote from his hospital bed.

> Never in my life have I thought I would
> write such a letter as this. The Boys' Home
> for which I have worked so hard and for so
> many years, must be closed unless the neces-
> sary money is raised immediately. If the
> home closes it will break my heart. That
> won't matter much. But it will break the
> hearts of these two hundred boys and deprive
> a chance in life to thousands of boys in the
> years to come. . . .

Small donations of cash, food, clothing and livestock somehow kept the home alive. Billy Capps stood in line with the others and cheered when Father Flanagan returned home. Billy's
grandmother did what she could. She wrote her grandson in
November of 1931.

> I just received your letter. I had a letter
> from your Daddy to you. Give the home $10
> and send me the rest for your sister Eleanor.
> Your daddy talked like he was going to get
> you but don't you go with no one or leave
> there until you hear from me.
> I hope you like it up there. Our priest
> thought it was such a nice place. Did you get
> the candy Rose sent? Now do as I tell you,
> don't you go with no one.

Billy was a good student. He got A's in art, grammar, agri-
culture, and geography. He loved to play baseball and other
sports. He went home for a visit in May of 1932. He intended to
come back to Boys Town in the fall, but he never made it. His
grandmother wrote Father Flanagan with the news.

> My Grandson, Billy Capps, had a very
> bad accident in July. He got caught in the belt

to a hay baler and almost lost his arm. The
doctor said it would take six months to heal,
so I won't know for a while what I can do
with him.

I will write you later. Thanks for everything.

Billy never did make it back to Boys Town. By the time his
arm finally healed he was almost 17. He decided to stay in
Kansas, but he never forgot Boys Town. He and Father Flanagan
kept up a correspondence for years. They wrote about what was
happening in their lives, about baseball, and about their hopes for
the future. For Billy Capps his future was war. It was in the
Philippines, in a place called Bataan, that Billy Capps would cross
paths with another Boys Town boy, Robert "Bobby" Paradise.

Bobby Paradise came to Boys Town from Long Pine,
Nebraska. In November of 1932, Bobby was brought for admission to Boys Town. His adopted father's health had deteriorated
and he could no longer take care of his son. Bobby moved to
Boys Town in December of 1932 while Boys Town was celebrat-
ing its fifteenth anniversary.

In February of 1933, there was a small article on Bobby in
Father Flanagan's Boys' Home Journal. ". . . If you were to look
into the big brown eyes of Robert Paradise you would see there a
sparkle that denotes energy and ambition. Robert just passed his
13th birthday on January 26, and his innate energy is expressed
in boyish pranks and sports.

"Robert loves music and since coming to the home has
taken up a band instrument and is a member of the third band
and also a member of the second chorus. He wants to learn to
play well enough to be one of the first band which broadcasts
over the radio each Sunday at one o'clock.

"Robert is a wholesome boy, preferring his school work,
music and athletics to anything else in his life. Every afternoon
he practices basketball and is always sorry when the practice
period is up."

He may have been "wholesome," but life wasn't always easy for Bobby. He missed his family. He left Boys Town twice in the first several months but returned both times. Eventually he thought of Boys Town as home and flourished. He enjoyed festivities like the Home's Fourth of July celebration in 1933. Activities included a baseball game, swimming, races, and a picnic with chicken, root beer, and ice cream. As a final treat, the boys all watched a Charlie Chaplin movie in the auditorium.

The summers of 1933 and 1934 brought heat, dust, and drought to Boys Town. The boys formed "water brigades" to save the crops but were only able to salvage part of them. Bobby's family was also going through hard times.

His father's health continued to deteriorate. In 1935, after three operations, Bobby's adopted father died of a brain tumor. Now Father Flanagan was the only father Bobby had.

In September of 1936, Bobby left Boys Town to work on a farm in Pocahontas, Iowa. A year later he came back to Boys Town determined never to leave again.

When he returned there were several new boys to meet, among them Robert Wiskochil. Robert had come to Boys Town from Texas in March of 1937. He had had some minor trouble with the law in his home town of Dallas. His father was a travelling shoe salesman so he wasn't home much to provide guidance for his growing son. The family hoped the disciplined atmosphere of Boys Town might be just the place for Robert.

The month after Robert arrived, Joe Louis, World Heavyweight Boxing Champ, visited Boys Town. Through the years the boys had developed a strong interest in boxing. Father Flanagan encouraged their interest for he felt it built character. Louis' visit sparked a strong surge in interest and soon there were impromptu boxing tournaments springing up all over the Home.

Sports were a very important part of the boys' lives at the Home. From boxing to baseball, basketball, football, and other sports it was a way for the boys to release energy and learn lessons in teamwork.

Robert was a tennis player and was also interested in football. He wrote his family about making the football team and his mother wrote back.

> We received your letters the past weeks. I hope you will do well in football and I know you can, so Daddy will be pleased with you. He told us so many nice things about you when he came back from his last visit. I suppose he will get you the things you asked for.
>
> I am mailing you a box tomorrow. You should take care of the candy and it should last you a long time. Daddy expects to be in Omaha the latter part of September or the first of October. Sorry we can't come up this summer, maybe we can in the fall or around the holidays. The weather is a little cooler this week. We have had a very hot summer. Just too hot to go any place.

The Boys Town football team was class "B" state champions in 1937. It was the second of three straight undefeated teams. Robert Wiskochil had indeed made his father proud.

Bobby Paradise turned 18 on January 26, 1938. It was to be a very big year for him and for Boys Town. *Father Flanagan's Boys' Home Journal*, listed Bobby in the January birthday column.

". . . Another adherent to the skating sport is 'Bobby' Paradise, but from what we've seen he does most of his skating on his left ear. 'Gotta learn don't I,' he explains. Bobby is in both choir and band and plays on the basketball team."

Robert Wiskochil also had a birthday that winter. Robert turned 17 in March of 1938. His father stopped by see him. He brought a pair of shoes for Father Flanagan and a birthday gift for his son. The *Boys' Home Journal* called Robert, ". . . One of our southern gentleman hailing from the Lone Star state. He is eagerly awaiting those balmy days of spring to do some 'lone starring' in the tennis tournament."

That same month, the advance team from Metro-Goldwyn-Mayer studios visited the Home. They were gathering background for a movie on Father Flanagan and Boys Town. They also brought a gift for Bobby and his friends on the basketball team: new team uniforms.

All the boys were excited about the possibility of a movie about their town. They looked forward to meeting the stars, Spencer Tracy and Mickey Rooney. In April, Father Flanagan travelled to Hollywood to meet with the producers of the movie and to help prepare Tracy and Rooney for their roles.

Robert Wiskochil wasn't around when they filmed the movie that made Boys Town a household word. He returned to Texas with his father in June of 1938. Rumblings of war were already being heard in Asia. The Japanese had sacked Nanking and were rolling south through China. It was a war that would sweep up Robert Wiskochil, Bobby Paradise, William Capps and so many other Boys Town boys. For Robert, a small dot of land in the middle of the Pacific was to be his future home. He would join the Marines on Wake Island.

Back at Boys Town, Bobby Paradise had developed political ambitions. He had long been a member of the police force at Boys Town and that summer he decided to run for Police Commissioner. When he won the election, *Father Flanagan's Boys' Home Journal* said, "Bobby attained the height of a 'copper's' dream. His faithfulness to duty and his kindly regard for the little fellows were doubtless the points in determining his victory."

Those were virtues that would serve him well in the troubled years ahead. Bobby Paradise graduated from Boys Town in December of 1938. But it was another December, three years later, that he would remember for the rest of his life.

The Japanese bombed the Philippines the same day they attacked Pearl Harbor. Since they were on the other side of the international dateline, it was December 8 in the Philippines.

Soon everything was in an uproar as Paradise, who was serving as a medic, and his friends scrambled for the expected invasion.

Billy Capps was also preparing for the imminent Japanese attack. He had been in the Philippines for several months as a member of an Infantry division. He had written to Father Flanagan about his army life; the boredom and heat and the bugs. It wasn't until the bombs fell that he learned about blood and fire and death.

The Japanese hit Clark Field in the Philippines several hours after they bombed Pearl Harbor. The Americans knew they were coming but in the end it didn't matter.

Reports of what had happened at Pearl Harbor had reached the Philippines by radio. The American planes, 35 bombers and 72 fighters, took to the air immediately. However, the Japanese assault was delayed by a dense fog, and the Americans returned to the ground. While the planes were being serviced, and the men being fed, the Japanese attacked. Almost 100 planes were destroyed in the air or on the ground.

The American habit of parking the planes in formation had made them an easy target for the Japanese bombs. Coming on the heels of the disaster at Pearl Harbor, this defeat was very demoralizing to the American forces in the Philippines. It forced them to abandon their plans of defending the invasion on the beaches and to move instead into prepared positions on Bataan and Corregidor.

General Douglas MacArthur, the commanding general of the Allied forces in the Philippines, had prepared concealed supply depots and hospitals in the jungles of Bataan and gun emplacements on the island fortress of Corregidor.

Billy Capps and Bobby Paradise were both sent deep into the jungle of Bataan. Cut off from contact with the outside world, they survived on hoarded supplies and fought a delaying action against the Japanese. They didn't know that the Americans were losing the war on all fronts. Guam had been captured and Wake Island was under siege. They were waiting for a rescue that would never come.

Halfway across the Pacific, expert gunner Robert Wiskochil was also waiting. Waiting for the order to open fire on the Japanese task force that was slowly approaching Wake Island. Waiting for a chance to avenge the friends he had lost to Japanese bombs and bullets in an earlier air raid.

Just as in the Philippines, the men on Wake Island had known the Japanese were coming but when the first attack came they were caught unprepared. The Japanese planes had slipped in under some low clouds and strafed the Wake Island airfield. Bombs scored direct hits on four planes and three more were destroyed by fire. Only four American planes remained to continue the fight.

Of the 55 officers and men in the area of the airfield, 23 were dead or dying and 11 more were wounded. Some of Wiskochil's friends were never found. They only found pieces.

But the Japanese had made one critical mistake. Their raid wasn't the complete success they thought it had been. Most of the soldiers, four of the planes and many of the big guns had survived the attack. Now they waited in the pre-dawn darkness for the Japanese ships to come into firing range.

The hours crept by: Two-thirty . . . three o'clock . . . .

Wiskochil waited with the others and his muscles ached from the tension. "They're getting closer. An awful lot of them," said the man to his right.

Four o'clock . . . four-thirty. The Japanese fleet sailed still closer. At five o'clock the advance ships were only four miles offshore.

BOOM!

Wiskochil heard the first Japanese shells landing above the sound of the surf. The shells sent geysers of sand exploding into the air and splinters of shredded trees whistling above his head. He waited for the Marine commander, Major Devereaux, to give the order to open fire.

Just after six o'clock the command came. In one exultant, glorious rush the American guns opened up.

The tension and the pent-up rage exploded with the sounds of the guns and Wiskochil heard himself screaming defiance at the Japanese.

It was all over in 45 minutes. The invading Japanese task force limped away. The enemy had lost two destroyers, one sunk by the American guns and one by a bomb from one of the American planes. Japanese Admiral Kajioka had lost at least 500 men and five of his remaining ships were heavily damaged.

There were no American casualties.

For the first time since Pearl Harbor the Americans had won a victory. They had sunk two ships and turned away an invasion force that vastly outnumbered them. It was December 11, and America finally had something to celebrate.

Wiskochil and his mates shouted and danced their victory. They showered each other with warm beer and grinned until the muscles of their faces ached. When Commander Cunningham reported the victory to headquarters in Pearl Harbor, he was asked if he needed anything. "Yes, send us more Japs," was the reply.

It was a short-lived celebration. At nine o'clock the Japanese bombers arrived for another raid.

It became routine. The Japanese would fly over, drop bombs and strafe the island. The Americans would fire back with everything they had. But everything they had became less and less, and the casualties started to mount. Wake Island's defenders' only hope was a rescue force from Pearl Harbor. As time went by, it became clear no rescue was coming.

It was two days before Christmas, 1941, and the troops and civilians that remained were scattered and cut off from each other. When the Japanese landing parties finally arrived they met spirited, but futile, opposition. Within a matter of hours, Cunningham and Devereaux were forced to surrender.

For Robert Wiskochil it must have seemed a bitter end. Wake Island's defenders had held out for two weeks against overwhelming forces and now all that was left was to count the bodies and submit to imprisonment. Nearly 80 civilians and 51 soldiers and sailors had been killed. Ninety-eight more would be brutally executed several months later by the Japanese and 115 died in Japanese prisoner of war camps.

Wiskochil had survived the bombs and bullets of Wake Island but he would not survive prison camp. The seventh Boys Town alumnus to die in the war, his death added another gold star to the Boys Town service flag.

In a letter dated August 22, 1943, Robert's father, Al Wiskochil, wrote Father Flanagan:

> Robert I. Wiskochil, my son, who was
> one of your boys, died in a Japanese prison
> camp today. He was a Marine on Wake Island.

"A Marine on Wake Island." That simple phrase resonates to a whole generation of Americans. To those that fought the war in the Pacific, it symbolizes the sacrifices required for a nation preparing for total war.

Bobby Paradise and Billy Capps were also part of that vanguard of men whose sacrifices provided time for the American war machine to reach its fearsome potential. While Robert Wiskochil was fighting his last battle on Wake Island, they were digging in on the Bataan peninsula and preparing for a long fight.

The Japanese had expected to quickly roll over the Philippines and then move on to prepare for the invasion of Australia. The Allied resistance at first shocked them, then it infuriated them. MacArthur's retreat to Bataan had made it impossible for them to use their numerical superiority effectively. They had to push the Americans and Filipinos out mile by hard-fought mile.

The daily routine of artillery shellings, airplane bombings, and attacks by ground forces took their toll on the Allied forces. Bobby Paradise was kept busy caring for the wounded.

The makeshift hospitals where he worked were crammed full of injured men with every square foot of space occupied. Medical supplies soon ran low, and surgical teams competed with each other to see which team could handle the largest number of patients.

On February 8 of 1942, Paradise wrote Father Flanagan:

> (Somewhere in Bataan). Censorship is strict so cannot write much. Here we are in the middle of a war and all is O.K. Don't worry.

Father Flanagan replied:

> We are praying for you to return back to the United States after this war is over hale and hearty, having done a great job.

By now Paradise and Capps were surviving on a daily ration of a slice of bread, two to eight ounces of rice and an ounce or two of sardines with a touch of evaporated milk. They were becoming weaker and tired easily. Wounded men could only be moved by stretcher, and men were dying because the weakened stretcher bearers could not get them medical attention quickly enough.

Each day the Japanese advances claimed more and more Allied casualties. MacArthur had based his defensive strategy on an eventual rescue force being sent by the United States Navy. The disaster at Pearl Harbor had made that impossible. On February 22, 1942, MacArthur was ordered to leave Bataan and flee to Australia. He left General Wainwright in charge of Allied forces but vowed, "I shall return."

On April 4, 1942, MacArthur ordered Wainwright to plan a massive breakout against the Japanese if food and ammunition got too low. Billy Capps, Bobby Paradise, and all their fellow soldiers were being told anything was preferable to surrender. However, faced with a rapidly deteriorating situation, the troops on Bataan did surrender on April 9, 1942.

That same day, across the Pacific, Father Flanagan was writing a letter to Billy Capps. It was full of news of Boys Town, a time and place so far away from the jungles of Bataan.

It has been some time since I have written you and I thought I would drop you a few lines at this time.

Everything is humming with activity here at Boys Town. I might add that I am feeling fine after my recent operation at the Mayo clinic and it sure feels good to be back on the job again.

We are planning to have a huge Victory Garden this year. In fact, it will cover about 40 acres. We hope to raise sufficient food to carry us through next winter if it is humanly possible. Of course, this will mean a lot of work, but the boys have been enthusiastic and have all volunteered to work in our Victory Gardens during the summer. I too plan to devote an hour each day to working in the garden.

Mr. Corcoran has arranged a fine baseball schedule for our high school team this spring. We feel we have an outstanding team this year.

I hope that you find this letter interesting. Please drop us a line at your convenience in the near future. We shall be very happy to hear from you. If you should have a photograph of yourself, send it along, possibly we could use it in the Boys Town Times.

Say your prayers and attend church regularly William. Be assured that we remember you in our daily prayers.

It was a letter that Billy Capps would never read. The day before Allied forces on Bataan surrendered, he was killed. Father Flanagan first heard the news many months later in a letter from Billy's grandmother, Mary Shores Clark.

> I wish to inform you Billy Capps, a one-time boy of yours, lost his life in action, April 8th in the battle of Bataan. My health broke when I lost Billy. Pray for him.

Father Flanagan's letter to Billy's grandmother revealed the sorrow he felt at hearing the grim news.

> It is with great sorrow that I read of the death of your grandson, Billy Capps, who lost his life in the battle of Bataan. He is the twentieth Boys Town boy to pay the supreme sacrifice during World War II.
> I want to extend to you, my dear Mrs. Clark, my sincere sympathy in the death of your grandson. While your heart and the heart of Billy's friends must be torn asunder because of this terrible tragedy — there still arises within you a pride that fills that great void, and I know, too, that you seek help and consolation from Him who is the great consolation of the world, and one, if we only seek His aid, will supply to us much consolation in our hour of sorrow.
> I know something about this great loss. Boys Town has lost 19 other wonderful boys and while perhaps you may think that, after all, these boys are not as close to me as they would be to a natural father, still, let me assure you, my dear Mrs. Clark, they are very close and I feel the loss of each and every one very deeply.

For Billy Capps and Robert Wiskochil the war was over.

For Bobby Paradise, it was just beginning. He, and thousands of other defenders of Bataan, were now prisoners of the Japanese.

There were around 70,000 men listed in the Allied forces on Bataan when General Wainwright surrendered. Two months later just over 54,000 remained. Some, like Billy Capps, died during the last days of battle; many died from disease and starvation in the camps, and 600 Americans and 8,000 Filipinos died during the walking slaughter known as the Bataan Death March.

Bobby Paradise was lucky. As a member of the medical corps he was sent ahead of the main body of men to prepare the prisoner of war camp for their arrival. He was not there when the march began but he was there for its finish.

Most of the men on the march had not eaten in a week. They were already tired and weak from months of a starvation diet. Many were wounded or suffering from tropical diseases and fevers. They were glassy-eyed scarecrows struggling just to take the next step — sixty-five miles of "one more step."

The men in the front of the march set a slow pace so the stragglers could keep up. Still, many fell by the wayside too exhausted to move. If they would not stand, an enemy bayonet made sure they could never rise again.

When the survivors finally arrived at Camp O'Donnell nine days later, Bobby Paradise was there to help. Like rows of ragged clothing walking by themselves, the survivors of the march were a caricature of life.

"It was heart-breaking," said Paradise later in an interview in the *Boys Town Times*. "Many weren't able to make it and those who did were so weak they were barely alive." He added that more than one soldier, seeing the camp and realizing the march was almost over, would say, "I've got to make it," and then would die from exhaustion before medical help could reach him.

Back home at Boys Town, Father Flanagan had added a gold star to the service flag. Paradise was officially listed as missing but everyone assumed he was dead. It wasn't until January of

1943 that Father Flanagan knew for sure that Bobby Paradise was alive.

It was a small, fill-in-the-blanks postcard, sent to Father Flanagan by the Japanese Imperial Army, that brought the welcome news. It read:

> I am interned in Taiwan. My health is
> usual. I am working for exercise. Please see
> that your health is taken care of. My love to
> you.
> Bob F. Paradise

Paradise's health was not "usual." Although he had missed the death march, the conditions in Camp O'Donnell were horrific. Prisoners were dying at an alarming rate. According to survivors, it was not unusual for gravediggers to collapse from exhaustion and be buried in the grave they had just helped to excavate. Fed almost totally on rice, many prisoners withered and died. On May 27, 1942 alone, 588 men perished.

There wasn't much Paradise and the other medical staff could do to help their fellow prisoners. General W.E. Brougher, imprisoned at Camp O'Donnell with Paradise, described the camp hospital in his memoirs.

"There was no water. There were no cleaning materials. . ., no medicine and no hospital equipment. There was no furniture in the building of any kind. No beds; no chairs. There were hundreds of patients there on the floor. Most of them were suffering from malaria, dysentery, or both.

". . . I saw the living alongside the dead under the buildings. They were put out there to die. When a case became hopeless, they would just move them out on the ground under the house, and the dead were lined up there already, and in many cases a living man, in the last stages of his disease, was just put there and died."

A few weeks after the soldiers had arrived at Camp

O'Donnell, the Americans were ordered to stand a routine inspection. Those that could not stand were allowed to lie down, but were told to lie at attention when the inspecting officer approached. One of the men had a broken collarbone and could not lie at attention. In retaliation, a Japanese lieutenant kicked him in the face.

For Paradise that was too much.

Maybe it was the years at Boys Town: the boxing tournaments organized by Father Flanagan to teach the boys courage and self-respect. Maybe it was the former Boys Town Police Commissioner sticking up one more time for "the little guy."

"I just lost my head I guess, and punched the Japanese lieutenant, " Paradise later recalled. "I knocked him down and he fell back several feet."

Six Japanese soldiers jumped Paradise and began beating him. He was stabbed through one hand with a bayonet and had a ragged gash torn across his left temple. The soldiers left him for dead, and he lay unconscious for 12 hours.

"Sometime during the night a colonel came and dragged me into his tent, " recalled Paradise. "They hid me there for thirty days until I recovered." When the high-ranking officers left Camp O'Donnell for Camp Karenko in Taiwan, Paradise went along as a colonel's orderly.

As he and the other soldiers marched toward the ships that would take them to Japan or Taiwan, there occurred an incident that General Wainwright would recall in his memoirs.

As the men marched by, forlorn and weary, a young Filipino boy began whistling *The Star Spangled Banner*. "A Japanese guard walked menacingly close to the kid," Wainwright recalled, "but he never missed a note, never faltered, until the whole line had passed."

Things were better at Camp Karenko for Paradise. There were some medical supplies, and the men were encouraged to cultivate small gardens to supplement their rations. However, food was still scarce, and one of the men's prime amusements was to have long conversations describing the best meal they ever ate.

The Japanese began letting some of the prisoners send out radio messages for propaganda purposes. A message from Paradise was picked up by radio operators on the West Coast and relayed to Father Flanagan.

> Thanks for the letters. Please let me
> have all the news. I am working in the hospi-
> tal and all is good, so no need to worry.
> Please notify Monsignor Flanagan that I am
> well.

Father Flanagan sent a copy of the *Boys Town Times* in his next packet to Paradise. Paradise said all the prisoners "read it avidly until it literally fell to pieces."

Things were moving fast now for Paradise. The war was raging all around him but he had very little information on its progress. Just rumors or stories that the Japanese felt were favorable to their cause. In a letter written in May of 1944 to Father Flanagan, Paradise wrote:

> Well another year has rolled around and
> all is well. I am working in the hospital and
> enjoy my work. Today is the second anniver-
> sary of the Fall of Bataan. I am in excellent
> health. See you in 1945.

Just before Christmas of 1944, another propaganda broadcast by the Japanese government was intercepted by West Coast ham radio operators. The message from Paradise was printed in the *Boys Town Times*.

> I received your letters and papers from
> Boys Town. Last Christmas I received 107 let-
> ters from friends all over America.

Our camp is beautifully located. We have
a lovely garden and get vegetables from it
regularly. We are well treated considering we
are prisoners.

I work in the hospital here and receive
pay for my work each month. We have a canteen and are able to buy things available in
the area of Taiwan.

Father, I received your parcel and
enjoyed it very much. I read in the prayer
books each day and get many happy thoughts
from them, which makes waiting for the end
of the war easier. Well Father, I wish you a
Merry Christmas and a glorious New Year.

It was a cruel hoax. Paradise received no pay for his work in
the hospital, there were no supplies available from the canteen
and most of the Red Cross parcels intended for the prisoners
were confiscated. Since being taken prisoner, Paradise had lost
60 pounds. In fact, he didn't even write the propaganda letters.

"Shortly after I came to Camp Karenko, I was visited by
several Japanese intelligence officers," recalled Paradise. "They
asked me if I was from Boys Town and if Father Flanagan was a
famous person in the United States. I answered yes to both questions and that's when they started writing the letters."

Paradise knew the war was going badly for the Japanese.
Prisoners were no longer allowed to read Japanese newspapers.

He and his fellow prisoners were moved to Camp Haito
and conditions worsened. Half of the 350 prisoners at Camp
Haito perished from starvation, disease, and abuse. "We suffered
from dysentery, malaria and beri-beri," Paradise told the *Boys
Town Times*. "There was no medicine."

"We prayed that the Americans would come soon," he said.
"We knew that if they didn't, it would be too late."

When they finally came, they dropped bombs on the camp.
Haito had to be abandoned, and the survivors were moved back

into the mountains. Sick and emaciated they travelled over eight miles along a steep mountain path, bringing only what they could carry on their backs.

They set up camp on a barren and exposed hilltop. To try and fight the cold, Paradise and the other prisoners built huts made out of the only material available, grass and bamboo. They planted a garden to provide some minimal food and struggled to stay alive for a few more weeks or days. They knew help would have to come soon.

One night, shortly after they got to the camp in the mountains, a camp guard came in and insisted Paradise accompany him to the quarters of an Allied officer. "The officer was choking to death," remembered Paradise. "I had to perform an emergency tracheotomy. I used a pocket knife, a fountain pen, and a sewing needle and thread to do the job. Thank God he survived my surgery."

The camp had held 250 men at one time. They were the survivors of all the other camps that had been abandoned. When Paradise was finally rescued, only he and eleven other men were still alive.

They heard their rescuers before they saw them. The noise of healthy men moving through the brush, talking and joking. The Marines had come, and they were free. "I can't describe how I felt," said Paradise. "It was unimaginable joy."

However, it wasn't over yet for Paradise. Shortly after he was rescued he was brought up on charges of spying and threatened with a court martial. "It was the propaganda letters the Japanese had written in my name that caused the trouble. The government wanted to make sure I was who I said I was. They took my fingerprints and shipped them back to the States to be verified by Father Flanagan. Of course, he cleared me right away. I heard he was furious. I had no more trouble."

Paradise got his first taste of meat in three years when the liberated prisoners were served fried eggs and hamburger steak aboard an American warship. He was given a quart of cream every day for six weeks, and he regained his strength and most of the weight he had lost.

Paradise arrived in Seattle on October 19, 1945, and was sent to Fort Lewis near Tacoma, to recuperate. From there he telegraphed Father Flanagan that he was safe and coming for a visit.

"Thank God for Bobby," said Father Flanagan when he received the telegram. "That is the best news we have had in many, many months. Our prayers have been answered."

After leaving the service, Paradise went on to a career in Hollywood. He worked behind the scenes on several TV shows including *The High Chaparral*, *Bonanza*, *Gunsmoke* and *The Brady Bunch*. He also had small acting roles in *Bewitched* and *Iron Horse*.

Paradise is retired now but he keeps busy as a civilian consultant for Veteran Affairs. He volunteers to help his fellow veterans in any way he can. He's come a long way since Boys Town and 1945 but he still feels a debt to the people who welcomed him home so many years ago.

He came home as a conquering hero. There was a parade for him through downtown Omaha and the boys at Boys Town prepared an elaborate reception for their returning hero.

There was no fanfare for Billy Capps or Robert Wiskochil.

In 1946, while on a tour of the Philippines to help the Filipino people set up orphanages, Father Flanagan searched for Billy Capps' grave. He found it on a hillside where thousands of small white crosses stood row by row, mute witnesses to man's inhumanity.

They never found Robert Wiskochil's final resting place. He lies somewhere in an unmarked grave, swallowed up by the jungle. So far from friends and family. Forgotten now.

But not Bobby Paradise. Bobby came home.

★ t h r e e ★

My Daddy's flag

The cloth was ragged and torn. The edges were frayed, and the color was fading. There were stains on the red and white stripes, and a jagged hole where a star used to be.

It had belonged to his father, and it was all that remained. For him, it was the anchor of his memory. It was his proudest possession.

James Burns was 14 when he and his brothers, Thomas and Edward, first came to Boys Town in May of 1935. Their mother had passed away the year before, and their father, a World War I veteran, had died the previous March.

The American Legion in Leavenworth, Kansas, had taken care of their father's funeral arrangements and brought the Burns brothers to the attention of Father Flanagan.

A neighbor drove them up to Nebraska, and they watched other boys running and laughing as they waited in the car. James was the oldest. His brother Edward was 10, and his brother Thomas was 6.

They walked into Father Flanagan's office for the interview with Edward in the lead. Thomas followed him carrying one shoe in his hand, and James brought up the rear, his arms wrapped around a brown paper package.

During the interview 6-year-old Thomas chattered happily. He told Father Flanagan his foot was sore and that's why he was only wearing one shoe. He said they had left some chickens in Kansas but a neighbor had promised to take care of them. Normally Boys Town wouldn't admit anyone as young as Thomas but Father Flanagan just couldn't separate him from his older brothers. This pleased Thomas and he told Father Flanagan he "didn't want to ever go away" from his brothers.

Edward told Father he liked to fish and he wanted to be a musician. With its fishing lake and its band program, Boys Town seemed like just the place for Edward.

Throughout the interview Father Flanagan eyed the package that James clung to so tightly. Finally he asked, "That must be something precious. What is it?"

"It's a flag," James replied. "It was my Daddy's flag. We got it from his coffin. He was a soldier."

At Boys Town, life was good for the Burns brothers. They had plenty of food to eat, clothes on their back, and a roof over their head. Best of all they were together. They spent that summer working and playing, and James began to excel at baseball.

In October of 1935, Thomas and Edward were adopted by a farm family in South Dakota; James stayed at Boys Town. The brothers missed each other and wrote often. Short notes from children learning to write.

> Dear James,
>   Mother gave us a watch and a knife. We
> have a Shetland pony.
>   Your Brothers

Edward and Thomas were building a new family. But James was their brother by blood and they would not forget him.

James became a star pitcher on the Boys Town baseball team. John Clupny, a classmate of James, remembers him as a "good student. He was a tall, thin beanpole who wanted to be a pitcher," said Clupny.

"I remember me and a couple of the other guys made him a uniform out of old pajamas. It was quite comical."

If he stayed at Boys Town long enough, every boy earned a nickname. For the tall, slender James it was "Porky."

In the September, 1937, issue of the *Boys Town Times*, Porky Burns was described as ". . . a lad with a grin as long as himself and he seems very eager to tell us something about himself. 'Oh, I'm going to be a gardener and a good one too, 'cause Uncle Jack (Boys Town gardener) says so.' James is the pitcher for the 'Nationals,' winners of the Junior All-Star game."

James "Porky" Burns lived at Boys Town for two more years. He fell into the rhythms of the place; work on the farm and picnics in the summer, football and school in the fall, snowball fights in the winter, and baseball in the spring. He learned to love his second home.

In November of 1939, he was placed with a Reverend O'Leary in Burchard, Nebraska, and finished high school there. And in the back of his mind was an idea.

"He always wanted to be a soldier," his brother Edward said years later. "Our father had been a soldier, and James wanted to be a soldier too."

In June of 1940, James wrote Father Flanagan asking for his help in joining the Army. He was six- foot-three and 160 pounds and he was ready.

My reason for wanting to join the Army
is the fact that my father was in the Army

for 30 years and he told me it was a good
place to be and I would like to take his
advice.

His father was five years in the grave but James had not forgotten. He remembered his father's stories and the crisp uniform
he wore on special occasions. He remembered his father's flag
and a promise made by a young boy.

With Father Flanagan's help, James Burns fulfilled his
promise. He was a soldier now.

In October of 1940, he wrote to Father Flanagan that he
was rated an "expert" with the .50-caliber machine gun, the
highest score in his section. Eventually Burns was stationed in
Fort Lewis, Washington, with the Seventh Infantry, and it was
there that he met an old classmate.

Dear Father,
I am a PFC now. I hope to become a corporal some day. I am making $41 a month
now, including shooting pay.
John Clupny is out here with me in the
same regiment, the Seventh Infantry. I met
him in a theater in Vancouver one night. I
thought I recognized him. I looked for awhile.
I got up, went out, came back and asked his
name and it was him. After the show we
walked around, had a hamburger and talked
things over. It was so good to see him.
We go on maneuvers to Hawaii next
month sometime for about 25 days. It's probably just a rumor but it may be true. That's
all I got to say now. Good luck and God bless
you all.

The next time Father Flanagan heard from Burns was May
of 1941. He wrote that war was approaching and he was sure to
be caught up in it.

> I am in California for the first time in
> my life. Out on a reservation with scorpions
> and rattlesnakes.
> Tony Villone (former Boys Town mayor)
> said he'll be stationed at Fort Ord, about 65
> miles north of here. I hope I'll get a chance to
> see him.
> I may soon be at war after President
> Roosevelt said last night in his speech that
> we're closer to war than ever before.

It was a prophetic statement. In December of that year Pearl Harbor was attacked, and America entered the war. It was a tumultuous time at Boys Town as well. The day after Pearl Harbor a group of boys, led by Boys Town mayor and native Hawaiian, Jimmie Ross, stormed into Father Flanagan's office demanding to be allowed to join the Army and fight the enemy.

Father Flanagan calmed the boys and asked that they wait until they graduated when they could better serve their country. It wasn't until March of 1943 that Jimmie Ross joined the Marines. He was sworn in at Boys Town as part of a national CBS radio program.

Around the same time on the West Coast, James Burns was getting ready to ship overseas.

> We are getting ready to sail on a trans-
> port here at Tacoma, Washington. . . starting
> tomorrow.
> I sent you a picture of my company here
> in the 7th Infantry. I am in the top row on
> the right. Can't tell where they might send
> us. I hope we don't have to go over there. If
> we have to I'm willing to go and hope that
> God is with me to help take the country back
> to peace again and for the world too.
> I hope to be back to see you and Boys
> Town again. Well, I guess that's all I got to
> say and God bless you and the boys at Boys
> Town. We'll fight to the end and make the
> world safe for democracy. 'V is for victory.'

James Burns' first action was in the Mediterranean. His Seventh Infantry was part of the American Fifth Army which invaded Sicily in July of 1943. Michael Chiningo, a war correspondent, was with the Seventh Infantry during the early hours of the invasion and he described the landing as surprisingly easy.

When Burns' regiment reached a railway station about a mile inland, the phone was ringing. Chiningo, who spoke fluent Italian, answered. It was the local Italian divisional commander who had been awakened by the sound of gunfire and wanted to know if the Americans had landed. Chiningo assured him they had not, and the general returned to bed.

An intricate deception by British intelligence had convinced the Axis that the invasion of Sicily was only a feint and the full-scale invasion would occur in Greece. As a result, the Allies were able to land in Sicily virtually unopposed. However, the Germans soon recovered and put up a stiff resistance as they retreated toward the straits of Messina and the boot of Italy.

On July 25, 1943, three weeks after the invasion of Sicily, Italian dictator Mussolini was deposed and imprisoned. Less than a month later, the Allies reached Messina and Sicilian resistance ended. With Sicily conquered, James Burns and the Fifth Army began preparing for the invasion of Italy.

On September 9, the Allies made an amphibious landing at Salerno. The minute the Fifth Army hit the beach the Germans opened fire with machine guns, artillery and mortars. Burns and his mates cut through the barbed wire and crawled to refuge among the sand dunes.

Enemy tanks helped keep the Americans pinned down until Naval gunfire drove the tanks back. The Fifth Army made slow progress but by September 11 they had expanded the beachhead and were on the road to Naples. On September 12 and 13 the enemy counterattacked and halted the Allies' progress. The fighting raged fiercely for several days but eventually the Germans withdrew and Naples was occupied by the Allies on October 1, 1943.

On October 9, James Burns wrote to Father Flanagan from Italy.

> It has been a long time since I have
> written. Been pretty busy these days and
> there are times we can't write letters at all.
> At the present time I'm in Italy not very far
> from the enemy lines. I have been wounded
> once, which was a minor wound and received
> a Purple Heart medal. I'll send it to you to
> keep for me until I get back to the States.
>   I got that wound from strafing planes. I
> was in my Jeep leading a convoy. This was in
> Sicily when this happened, but I am still kick-
> ing yet. There is a rumor that one per cent of
> the men awarded with medals will go back to
> the States but I doubt it. Well, so long for now
> Father.

The next battle for Burns and the Seventh Infantry regiment was at the Volturno River. They would lead the attack on
the German positions on the north side of the river. The
American commanders planned to make a feint on the left flank
while they sent the Seventh Infantry to lead the main assault in
the center.

The Volturno River valley was sliced by small streams and
sunken roads. Orchards, vineyards, and fields of grain dotted the
landscape.

In normal times the Volturno flows gently with many easy
crossing points. Unfortunately, days of heavy rains had turned it
into a maelstrom of muddy foam and floating logs. It was almost
300 feet wide and over six feet in depth. The rain had turned the
river's steep banks into greasy ten-foot mud slides.

Shortly after midnight on October 13, the Seventh Infantry
began moving into position to cross the Volturno. Burns and his
mates slogged through the wet countryside, pausing now and
again to retrieve a boot yanked off a marching foot by the suck-
ing mud.

A full moon brightly illuminated the scene, assisted by brilliant flashes of light as the American artillery laid down a withering barrage on the German positions. Blazing red tracers exploded from the American side and bounced off the German positions across the river. Faint white tracers from the enemy replied sporadically. Burns may have been reminded of the July Fourth celebrations back at Boys Town but his reverie was shattered by the sound of the guns and the deadly effect he knew they were having.

Author Richard Tregaskis, in his book, *Invasion Diary*, described the bombardment he witnessed. "Our barrage continued undiminished. The shells were like plucking hands; it seemed that they must be pulling the enemy hills to pieces."

At 2:00 a.m. the Seventh Infantry reached the river and began crossing the Volturno in life rafts, assault boats, and life-preservers. Smoke shells were fired to obscure their passage but they were soon spotted by the Germans and were targeted by the enemy machine guns. With machine gun bullets ripping into the water, the rafts and the boats, Burns and his mates paddled frantically across the flooded Volturno.

The soldiers emerged dripping from the water and scrambled up the slippery river banks to throw themselves at the enemy. Bright flares curved into the night-sky and fell backwards. The blood of the wounded and dying mixed with the mud and river water.

The last troops were across by dawn and were able to repulse an attack by enemy tanks. By the end of the afternoon, the Seventh Infantry had taken the heights that dominated the river on the German side. Other units had also accomplished their objectives.

But at what a cost! There were almost 400 Allied casualties suffered in the assault on German lines. Somewhere in the mud and the water James Burns had fallen. He had died a soldier's death, fighting for a cause he believed in, surrounded by his friends.

Ironically, Italy had declared war on Germany the same day that James Burns was killed.

Father Flanagan heard the news from the Buckleys who had adopted James' brothers, Edward and Thomas.

> We are sending you sad news. Eddie & Tommy received word from the war department that James G. Burns was killed in action in Italy on October 13th, 1943.

Father Flanagan wrote back to the Buckleys.

> . . . Your letter telling me the sad news of the death of James Burns was really a shock to us. I had just had a nice letter from him written on October 9th, only four days before he was killed. It seems we are losing so many of our boys.
>
> Please extend to Eddie and Thomas my sincere sympathy. I know this news has been a shock to them. I hope they will be able to visit us sometime.

Edward and Thomas Burns, in their sixties, still think about the brother they lost so many years ago.

Thomas was so young his memories of his brother are vague, but Edward remembers him clearly. They never saw James again after they were adopted and moved to South Dakota. "He was going to come and visit us on a furlough before he went overseas," said Edward, "but for some reason he never made it."

"They sent us his Purple Heart Medal," Edward added. "He was so proud of being a soldier. He wanted our father to be proud of him."

When asked if he still had his father's flag Edward responded, "That old flag of our father's was made out of wool and the moths got to it. Nothing left now.

"They did send us the flag from James' coffin though. We

still have it in the attic in a cedar chest I bought overseas. I look at it every now and then. My wife asks me about James some- times but I don't know what to tell her. It all seems so long ago now."

★ four ★

Just Kat

There is a narrow road that winds outside the village of Bruyeres in southern France. Called the Rue du 442e, it is named for the Japanese-Americans who liberated this small town in World War II. By the road side there is a modest rectangular plaque that reads, "To the men of the 442nd Regimental Combat Team, U.S. Army, who reaffirmed a historic truth here – that loyalty to one's country is not modified by racial origin. . . . "

Katsu Okida was one of the men of the 442nd who fought to liberate that small village in France. Before he went overseas, he lived for a time in another small village. This one was in Nebraska, a place called Boys Town.

There is an old photograph of Katsu Okida in Boys Town's files that catches the eye. He is dressed in fatigues carrying his backpack and bedroll with a rifle slung over his shoulder. He is looking back and the sun is in his eyes. The shadow from his helmet reaches past the bridge of his nose. Behind him are rows of barracks and a lone pine tree. Written with precise penmanship are the words "To Father" in the upper left-hand corner and "Just Kat" in the lower right-hand corner.

He stands there like a man with something to prove. Something he never thought he'd have to prove; that he was just as good an American as anyone else.

Katsu Okida was a Nisei, a second-generation Japanese-American. He, Peter Okada, and Patrick Okura and his wife Lily were among several Japanese-Americans brought to Boys Town by Father Flanagan during World War II. The story of how they came to Boys Town begins on December 7, 1941.

"I was 20 years old and living in California," said Peter Okada. "It was a Sunday and as I was walking out of church people were talking excitedly in small groups about the attack on Pearl Harbor. I thought, where is Pearl Harbor? It seemed so remote and far away. I never thought it would touch me.

"I had planned to go fishing that day and as I walked to the ocean people would stop and stare at me, then glare and curse. When I got to the coast, I could see the Army moving artillery into the tomato fields. Then I realized, 'this is serious,' and I turned around and went home."

Patrick Okura was on a golf course with his father-in-law on December 7, 1941. They endured the stares of the other golfers, cut their game short and headed home.

"It was like a siege mentality," Okura recalled more than 50 years later. "The streets were deserted, and everyone stayed home with their family. That night the FBI came and raided our part of town. They picked up 2,000 men, including my father, and took them to holding camps. We didn't see my father for two-and-a-half years."

Okura's father had come to America in 1905. At that time most Asian immigrants were ineligible for citizenship. It wasn't until 1952 that Okura's father and thousands of other Asian-

Americans listed as residents were made eligible for citizenship.

In January of 1942, the campaign for evacuation of the Japanese-Americans on the West Coast got under way. Henry McLemore, a columnist for the *San Francisco Examiner*, was typical of many editorial writers during this time. "... Does the government feel the lovely California climate has changed them and that the thousands of Japanese who live in the boundaries of this state are all staunch and true Americans?

"I am for the immediate removal of every Japanese on the West Coast to a point deep in the interior. Herd 'em up, pack 'em off and give 'em the inside room in the Badlands. Let 'em be pinched, hurt, hungry and dead up against it."

In the days after Pearl Harbor, the fact that most of these people he was recommending for removal were American citizens didn't seem to matter.

On February 19, 1942, President Roosevelt signed Executive Order #9066 which authorized the removal of Japanese-Americans to evacuation centers. Patrick and Lily Okura, Peter Okada, and Katsu Okida were sent to the Santa Anita racetrack. They were held there, with thousands of other Japanese-Americans, until permanent camps could be built.

Patrick's wife, Lily, was the secretary for E.J. England, one of the administrators at the camp. England had contact with the Maryknoll Fathers who also corresponded with Father Flanagan. When the Maryknoll Fathers told Flanagan about the treatment of the Japanese-Americans, Flanagan offered employment and living accommodations for up to eight Japanese families if they would come to Boys Town.

In his application to Father Flanagan, Katsu Okida wrote:

> I know this is an opportunity for me if I
> can qualify for the job. Even if I cannot go, it
> is certainly heartening to know of someone
> who has taken an interest during these trying
> times.

According to Patrick Okura, Father Flanagan was way ahead of his time. "He was offering employment and living quarters for Japanese-Americans two years before the American government did. He was a man of strong convictions, and he thought what was happening to us was wrong. He was determined to do whatever he could to help."

Patrick and Lily were the last people to leave Santa Anita. They had been in contact with Father Flanagan and had made plans to come to Boys Town as soon as possible. Unfortunately, they had trouble getting permission to travel to Nebraska and were getting on the train that would take them to a relocation camp in Arkansas when a soldier ran up waving a message.

"He said, 'I'm looking for an 'Irishman' named Patrick Okura, I have travel permits for him,'" recalled Okura. "Instead of boarding the train for Arkansas, we got on one for Omaha."

Peter Okada learned about Father Flanagan and the work at Boys Town from Patrick and Lily. He asked, "Who's he and where's that?" Then he sent his application to Boys Town but was sent to Amache relocation camp in Colorado before he heard back from Father Flanagan.

"Father Flanagan's letter was forwarded to me in Amache and he said, 'Please come,'" said Okada. "I asked if I could stay in Amache for two weeks to make some furniture for my mother. The barracks she was living in was just bare walls, no furniture, no nothing. There was a barbed wire fence around the camp and guards in watchtowers. I worked day and night to make furniture for my mother, and then I got out of that place."

Katsu Okida also heard about Boys Town at Santa Anita. He was already at Boys Town when Patrick, Lily, and Peter arrived.

Katsu Okida was hired by Boys Town as a carpenter. He had learned the trade working as a ship's carpenter on tuna boats in California. He was a well-known figure in his town of Terminal Island, a small village of Japanese immigrants.

"Kats worked on the tuna clippers and was gone for months at a time," recalled Peter Okada. "All the crew members shared in the profits of the catch, so Kats did pretty well. I remember him riding around on a motorcycle and wearing tailor-made clothes. He had even visited Hollywood, something that most of us had never done.

"When I got to Boys Town, Kats was already here, we shared rooms. I remember being surprised by Boys Town. I had expected high walls and bars on the windows, but it was like a college campus, peaceful and quiet. However, I did discover they had their own special rules and regulations.

"The place was governed in part by the boys. They had their own court and their own punishments. I remember hearing that one boy who broke the rules was being sentenced to the 'movie' punishment. Now going to the weekly movie on campus was something all the boys really enjoyed so I didn't understand the sentence until I went to the show. The boy being punished had to sit with his back to the movie while everyone else got to enjoy it. It was very effective."

Peter Okada was hired as a gardener and a part-time driver. Patrick and Lily Okura were hired to work in the welfare department. While Peter and Katsu lived on campus, Patrick and Lily tried to find a home in Omaha.

"I'd call and make an appointment to see the real estate agent," said Patrick. "They were always friendly on the phone. I guess they thought I was Irish. But when they'd meet me face to face they'd say, 'Oh I'm sorry, we just sold that house.' After about the fifth time it happened, I challenged the real estate person and they said, 'Leave my office, I'm a Christian.' And I said, then why don't you act like a Christian?"

Eventually the same law firm that worked for Boys Town took Okura's case to court and he was finally able to buy a house in 1944. Shortly after buying the house, Okura brought his family out of their relocation camp to live with him in Omaha. After the war, he stayed on at Boys Town as a psychologist. He would remain at Boys Town for 17 years.

In contrast, Peter and Katsu only lived at Boys Town for about a year. However, in that time they became an integral part of the campus and considered it home. They became just two more of Father Flanagan's "boys."

Peter Okada remembers his year at Boys Town as "one of the best years of my life. They treated me so well," he said. "I had left a younger brother behind at the relocation camp, and I was concerned about him. When I told Father Flanagan about it, he asked me why I hadn't said something about it earlier. He told me to send for him and I did. My younger brother ended up graduating from Boys Town High School."

Katsu and Peter became good friends and Peter remembers their friendship fondly. "Katsu could do so many things," he recalled. "He was a hunter and a marksman, and he had a real love and knowledge of music. He loved to carve wood. I remember he went to Omaha and bought a piece of mahogany wood and carved a ballerina for the daughter of one of the other employees."

In February of 1943, something happened that would take Katsu and Peter away from Boys Town.

After Pearl Harbor was bombed, many Japanese-Americans already in the armed services had their weapons taken away and were reassigned to KP and digging latrines. Japanese-Americans who tried to join the armed services to fight for their country were denied entry.

In February of 1943, President Roosevelt announced the formation of the 442nd Infantry Regimental Combat Team to be comprised of Americans of Japanese ancestry.

He said no loyal citizen of the United States should be denied the right to fight for his country. The call went out to over 110,000 Japanese-Americans in relocation camps across the United States. The response was overwhelming. In Hawaii alone, they had 10,000 volunteers for 1,500 roster slots.

However, the Army was still suspicious of Japanese-Americans. On the day that the 442nd entered their barracks in Camp Shelby, Mississippi, as full-fledged American soldiers, General DeWitt, commanding general of the Western Defense Command, said, "A Jap is still a Jap. They are a dangerous element. There's no way to determine their loyalty."

Ken Kawami, who began working at Boys Town shortly after the war, served with Katsu Okida in the 442nd. "We had to fight the Germans, and we had to fight American discrimination," he recalled. "But we discovered that when machine gun bullets and shells are going overhead, we're all human beings. Everyone is scared."

Late in the summer of 1943, Katsu and Peter left together to join the service and fight for their country. They were scheduled to go to Camp Shelby to join the 442nd when Peter Okada had second thoughts.

"I was the oldest of four sons," Okada said. "We had lost our father when I was only nine, and my mother had tried to make up for his absence by teaching us about Japanese culture and history. I was very curious about Japan and wanted to go there someday.

"While waiting to go to Camp Shelby and the 442nd, I found out about a secret operation in Camp Savage, Minnesota, called the Military Intelligence Language School. They were looking for people who spoke Japanese. I passed the test to go to Camp Savage and went there instead of Shelby. We were going to be used to help translate and to interrogate prisoners.

"After going through months of extensive training, I was shipped out to the Philippines. We were zig-zagging across the Pacific when they dropped the bomb on Hiroshima. By the time I got to the Philippines, Japan had already surrendered. I stayed on in the Philippines for a while and then went to Japan to serve with the American occupation forces."

Okada was destined to see Father Flanagan again when

Flanagan visited Japan after the war. They had a warm meeting with photographs and newspaper stories chronicling the reunion of Father Flanagan and one of his "boys."

Like his friend Peter Okada, Katsu Okida kept in contact with Father Flanagan. He wrote to Flanagan from the induction center in Salt Lake City, Utah, shortly before he joined the 442nd Combat Team.

> Please forgive me for this belated letter. I have been on the go ever since I left Boys Town. Now I am waiting to be inducted or sworn in.
>
> I made a visit to Los Angeles and now I am here in Salt Lake City. I was very disappointed in not being able to get into the Naval forces I had applied for. Despite the fact that I had many years of sea experience and have held masters papers for small craft. Even with the urgent need of small craft experienced men, I was told I could not enter the Naval service because I wasn't born of the right parentage. However, I shall be accepted in the Army.
>
> . . . Before I join my unit, I have to attend to some business concerning my folk's home in Los Angeles that has been ransacked by vandals.
>
> I certainly miss all of you. Please tell my friends that I am alright.

Okida went through basic training and remained at Shelby with the 442nd until they boarded troop ships for Europe in May of 1944. The trip by boat took almost a month and the 442nd disembarked in Naples and moved north of Rome to confront the Germans on the Gothic line.

Okida served with many men he had grown up with. They had been in the internment camps and basic training together. They were patriotic Americans who wanted to defend their

country, and finally, they were being given a chance. To symbol-
ize their attitude, they chose "Go For Broke" as their regimental
motto.

One of the men in Okida's outfit was "Babe" Okura the
younger brother of his old friend from Boys Town, Patrick Okura.

"I remember Katsu writing and telling me not to worry, he
would take care of my little brother for me," recalled Okura.
"Katsu was 27 and most of the other guys in his outfit were
teenagers like my brother. I had to laugh when I got a letter from
my little brother saying, 'There's some old geezer in this outfit
named Okida who wants to tell me what to do.'"

Father Flanagan's next letter from Okida was written June
24, 1944 from "somewhere in Italy."

> I presume a great many of the boys
> have reached the age to enter the service and
> new ones are coming in to fill their places. I
> hope we can bring this fracas over soon so
> those entering the service now, need not have
> to go through this which we are experiencing.
> I cannot write as much as I would like
> to, due to our own security at present.
> Perhaps I can write more later. One thing
> which I enjoy is the travel and seeing at least
> part of the world, which, in normal times, I
> would never have seen. This, in itself, is very
> interesting, to see how the other people live.
> I find though, that all people are the
> same, living only in a different environment
> with another tongue.
> I hope you are in the best of health and
> that everything is alright at Boys Town. I
> hope we can come home soon. How I wish I
> could be home now. Goodbye and God bless
> you Father.

Two days after he wrote this letter, Okida's company of
nearly 200 men was lured into an enemy trap and suffered so

many casualties that it was considered unfit for fighting as a unit for some time afterward. Okida himself was wounded and sent his next letter to Father Flanagan just after he left the hospital where he had been recuperating.

> I found your letter waiting for me upon my return from the hospital. How good it was to hear from you. Since my last writing I have been in some bitter fighting and in several instances I have been very close to being killed. But I presume the good Lord put an invisible shield around me.
>
> I tell you Father, there isn't a single atheist up here on the front lines. If anyone has never prayed before, he certainly does up here.
>
> I was very much delighted to have you send me the Boys Town Times. I find it especially interesting to find news about the boys who I know. Please give my best regards to everyone there. And I would be very much obliged if a few prayers could be said for our boys here and in return, I promise I'll say some prayers for you.

In September of 1944, Katsu and the 442nd set sail for the newly opened front in France. They arrived at the Vosges mountains in southern France the second week of October.

The area was heavily wooded, dank, and dark. Even at midday the sun barely filtered through the tangle of branches. Night in these woods was as black as a pit with no moon or stars visible. The men of the 442nd stumbled through the woods leaning on the shoulder of the soldier in front of them.

In this world of half-light the Germans had skillfully hidden machine gun nests and dugouts. They were camouflaged so well, the men of the 442nd could easily blunder into their line of fire.

Major General John Dahlquist, commander of the 36th Division, told the commander of the 442nd that the regiment would have an easy time; there was no sign of the enemy in the Vosges forest. On October 15, the 442nd began to advance into the forest. General Dahlquist expected them to make six miles a day. The first day they made 150 yards.

The enemy was entrenched and lying in wait for the Americans. Machine-gun fire and shelling took their deadly toll, but it was a new form of terror dubbed "tree bursts" that had the most horrific effect. When shells hit the tops of the densely packed trees, they exploded into lethal slivers of wood. It multiplied the destructive power of the shells. Even foxholes were not a safe haven unless they had a heavy cover on them.

It was turning colder in the forest, and the rain continued unabated. Foxholes filled with water before they were even completely dug out. The men of the 442nd began to suffer from trenchfoot which left them unable to walk.

On the morning of October 17, an enemy counterattack brutalized and decimated Okida's Company F. It was the second time in less than six months that he had watched many of his friends wounded and killed. The company reformed and closed ranks but they were fewer, weary and wounded.

The next day members of the 442nd liberated the small town of Bruyeres. They took 134 enemy prisoners. The villagers were amazed at the Japanese-Americans. They had not expected their rescuers to be Orientals. They had never seen Americans who looked like these men did.

On October 25, the First Battalion of the 36th Division's 141st Infantry Regiment, consisting of 275 men, was cut off and surrounded by the German army in the Vosges forest. The 442nd, battle-worn and exhausted, was ordered to mount a rescue operation. They had to save the "Lost Battalion."

The enemy did not attack in force because they were uncertain of the number of American soldiers they had trapped.

As the 442nd advanced through the dim forest, it became obvious that the German lines were wrapping ever tighter around the Lost Battalion. Several hundred elite German soldiers, trained for mountain warfare, had been sent in to reinforce their existing troops.

On October 27, the enemy launched a counterattack that stopped the 442nd in its tracks. The shelling and the heavy machine-gun fire drove them to the ground and Okida and his mates dug makeshift foxholes to protect themselves. They would get no closer that day.

The men in the Lost Battalion had been trapped for several days and their supplies were running low. An artillery shell packed with chocolate was fired into their perimeter by the Americans but it was buried so deep in the rain-soaked soil that the men couldn't get to it.

The men of the Lost Battalion dreamed of food, hot and fresh. Steak and eggs and pancakes and fresh milk. They argued about the best meal they ever had. They dealt with their hunger by recalling past feasts. And they waited. Waited for the rescue that had to come.

On Sunday, October 29, Okida awoke to fog and rain. Another miserable day in the Vosges forest. At least he had food; cold and greasy, but food nonetheless. This day they would assault one of the hills that separated them from the Lost Battalion.

The Germans had the advantage as they fired down the hill at the advancing Japanese-Americans. The machine-gun bullets seemed to come from everywhere. There was no safe place, and the lists of the wounded and the dead grew hour by hour.

Company K and Company I were in the forefront of the assault on the hill and they were taking the brunt of the casualties. In frustration and fear, one of the soldiers let out a scream of defiance as he ran from tree to tree up the hill. As if by mass hysteria, the rest of the soldiers began to yell as they advanced into the hail of machine-gun bullets and the deadly shell-bursts.

The survivors remember it as the "Banzai Charge." It had no organized beginning. It began and it grew fueled by rage at the death and the maiming of good friends and companions. So many lost, so many hurt. Building, pulsating with its own terrible life. A thing of rage that reached the crest of the hill and exploded against the dazed German defenders.

The "Banzai Charge" was not without cost. Many fell on their way up the hill. Doc Miyamoto, a medic in the 442nd, remembers hearing one of his wounded comrades whisper, "Kachan, itai, itai" (Mama, it hurts, it hurts).

They were closer now. They could see the Germans were pulling back very gradually. That night, as Okida rested, it was cold and dark. There was ice in the bottom of his foxhole. Maybe tomorrow they would break through. Tonight it was time for thoughts of home.

A week earlier he had found time to scribble a quick note to Father Flanagan.

> I hope everything is fine and the new building program is under way. I am fine and carrying on as best I can.
> We are in France, exactly where and what we are doing I cannot say at present. France is beautiful and the people are friendly and cordial.
> I presume Boys Town is the same, boys come and go. But with the expansion program, a little change may come. Well Father, I shall say so long for now. I know you and Boys Town are keeping us all in your prayers. And I too pray for an early reunion in a better world. My regards to you all and God be with you.

It rained the morning of October 30, and the men of the Lost Battalion shivered in the cold mist. Their supplies and ammunition were low. They braced themselves for a final attack.

It came with a brutal fury. The Germans attacked on three sides of the battalion's broken perimeter. The 141st fought back with everything they had, not worrying about rationing ammunition. They knew if this attack was not turned back it would all be over quickly.

It was when they heard the sound of firing from behind them that they almost gave up hope. The survivors turned to face this new threat. But what emerged from the mist were friends, not enemies.

"It was the Japanese-Americans who broke through the enemy and saved us," said Sergeant Bill Hull, a member of the Lost Battalion. "I was giving thanks to God and that Japanese-American soldier looked real special to me."

Members of Company I were the first to break through. They were mobbed by the Lost Battalion. Henry Nakada of Company I jumped into a soldier's foxhole. The man hugged him and began yelling at the top of his voice. Other survivors celebrated their deliverance joyfully.

For the men of the Lost Battalion, it was over. They walked back down the hill to hot food and clean clothes. The war correspondents were waiting for them. The 442nd stopped only briefly. They continued to pursue the enemy. General Dahlquist had ordered them to take the next hill.

The 442nd continued to advance against the enemy. They were the victims of daily shellings and bomb runs. By November 1 the Third Battalion of the 442nd was down to a quarter of its regulation strength. Those who were left plodded on without relief, watching their numbers dwindle and fade. Katsu Okida's Company F was down almost two-thirds in strength.

Okida himself was weary but alive. He had made it this far through luck, skill, and a tenacious will to survive. Through the bloody Italian campaign to the horrors of the Vosges forest he had endured. He was sure the order to turn back would come soon. Surely General Dahlquist could see the 442nd was on its last legs.

Babe Okura was gone. Killed in a mortar attack when he was crowded out of his foxhole by a lieutenant who had no foxhole of his own. Lying partially exposed, Babe Okura was butchered by flying shrapnel. Okida had not been able to protect his friend Patrick's little brother.

The 442nd had rescued the Lost Battalion but still General Dahlquist insisted they press on. On November 6, 1944, luck finally ran out for Katsu Okida who was killed during an artillery shelling by the enemy.

That night the first snow of winter fell. It drifted into the hollows of the hills and melted into the standing water in the bottom of empty foxholes. Painting the forest in shades of black and white, it covered up the dead and dying, a soothing white shroud that hid the horrors of war.

On November 9, the orders to pull back finally came. Too late for Katsu Okida, Babe Okura, and hundreds of other young men. On November 12, when the 442nd lined up for inspection by General Dahlquist, he turned to Lieutenant Colonel Miller of the 442nd and declared angrily, "I ordered that all the men be assembled."

"Yes sir," replied Colonel Miller. "All the men are what you see." The regiment had dwindled to less than a third of its regulation strength.

The 442nd Regimental Combat Team had survived, but just barely. It was the most highly decorated unit in World War II. No other unit equalled its record for tenacity or valor.

Several years after the war, Colonel Singles, the commander of the 442nd, met General Dahlquist at a military ceremony. Dahlquist offered his hand and said, "Let bygones be bygones. It's all water under the bridge, isn't it?"

Colonel Singles who felt the 442nd had been badly used by Dahlquist, ignored the general's extended hand. He looked straight ahead and stubbornly continued to hold his salute.

Patrick, Lily, and Babe Okura, Peter Okada and thousands of other Japanese-Americans, all fought to be recognized as citizens who were deserving of the same rights of citizenship as all other Americans.

And Katsu Okida, the man who carved wooden ballerinas, dressed in tailor-made clothes and entered the Army at age 26 to fight for his country, was an appropriate symbol for all of them. Even to his name, "Katsu," the Japanese character or word, that translates as "to gain a victory."

Korean War

The United States had enjoyed nearly five years of peace following World War II when Communist North Korea invaded South Korea. On June 27, 1950, President Truman ordered American forces into the conflict, a war that would last three years and claim more than 54,000 American lives.

Again, young men from Boys Town answered the call; dozens served overseas and at least six were killed in action.

Boys Town underwent many changes in the years before war broke out in Korea. By far the biggest involved the leadership of the Home. In May 1948, while on a goodwill visit to Germany, Father Flanagan was stricken with a heart attack and died. The visit was one of many Father Flanagan made to foreign countries after World War II to share his ideas on the care of children. A growing Boys Town welcomed Monsignor Nicholas Wegner as its new executive director.

Under Monsignor Wegner's guidance, the Home continued to grow in size and in national prominence.

The Korean conflict is sometimes known as "the forgotten war." Although it was the first test of America's promise to protect its Asian allies against communism, it did not have the global impact that World War II had. But the sacrifices of the men who fought there, and especially those who died, were as great as those of any soldier in any war.

As comrades-in-arms, the men of Boys Town once again served proudly.

★ f i v e ★

Pride of the Corps

Marine Sgt. Bob Mitchell peered out of his trench into the inky Korean night. Squinting, he tried to pick up any movement below his position on a rocky mound known as Bunker Hill. Mitchell and the other men of Easy Company knew the enemy was out there — the Chinese infantrymen, crawling up close, waiting for the flares and bugles that would signal the start of the attack.

The Marines had captured the hill from the Chinese a few days earlier. Now the Chinese wanted it back, and Mitchell's company had been ordered to hold it. His squad was in a forward trench, just below the crest; when the enemy's charge came, Mitchell's men would get hit first.

Mitchell had already seen his share of combat. A Marine for four years, this was the 21-year-old's second tour of duty in Korea. He had waded ashore at Inchon in the brilliant amphibious landing that cut off the invading North Korean forces and sent them fleeing north. Mitchell's division had fought house-to-house in the towns and villages, recapturing the South Korean capital of Seoul and pushing north, deep into North Korea, to the Chosin Reservoir. When 130,000 Chinese troops attacked U.S. and United Nations forces in November 1950, Mitchell was among the 15,000 Marines and U.N. troops who fought their way out of the rugged mountains to safety.

In spring 1951, he was wounded in the leg by machine gun fire and spent nearly four months in a hospital bed back in the United States. He volunteered for a second tour of duty and returned to Korea in 1952.

Now, on this desolate hillside, he whispered last-minute instructions to his men — "Stay down. Wait for the order to open fire."

As the seconds ticked by, Mitchell thought about home. Boys Town seemed a million miles away.

Bob Mitchell was 14 when he arrived at Boys Town in 1945. He had spent most of his childhood in an orphanage in St. Joseph, Missouri, where his father had placed him and the other five children in the family after their mother died in 1936. Bob's two older brothers, Charlie and James, had been sent to Boys Town before him, and it seemed only right that he follow them there.

Boys Town was good for Bob. He studied the printing trade and excelled in sports, lettering in football, basketball, track, baseball, and boxing. He got to travel with the football team when it toured the country playing high school teams in other cities. Bob got his first airplane ride when the team played a Miami high school one year. He also got to know Father Flanagan, whom he considered one of the greatest men he ever met. And he learned the value of hard work, good character, and discipline. Bob would later call his time at Boys Town as "one of the best deals of my life."

Bob made a lot of friends at Boys Town. One of them was Herbie Werner, a kid from New Jersey. When Bob left the Home and joined the Marine Corps in 1948, Herbie decided to go along. They went through boot camp together, and when the Korean War started, their division was among the first sent overseas.

As Mitchell nervously waited in the dark trench, he wondered if he would ever see his friend or Boys Town again.

Suddenly, a red flare lit up the night sky.

You might call it a quirk of fate.

It was late May, 1948. Father Flanagan had died a few weeks earlier in Germany, during a tour of Europe. His body had been brought back to Boys Town and laid to rest in Dowd Memorial Chapel.

About the same time, 17-year-old Bob Mitchell had decided to leave Boys Town and join the Marines. He had been staying at his father's house in Omaha, and now was back on the Boys Town campus to gather his belongings.

In Building Four, the dormitory where Bob lived, he ran into Herbie Werner. Herbie, who had come to Boys Town from Newton, New Jersey, the same year Bob arrived, had heard his friend was leaving.

"What are you going to do, Bob?"

"I joined the Marines."

"Well, do you think they'd take me?"

"I don't see why not."

Herbie and Bob both had dreamed of being soldiers. They had seen the former Boys Town kids return from World War II with their snappy uniforms and had listened to their stories. Herbie even had slept in a Marine barracks and talked to Guadalcanal veterans when he was on tour with the Boys Town Choir.

Herbie and Bob talked a while longer about the Marines.

Then Herbie made a decision — he would meet Bob at the Omaha recruitment office and join up, too.

A few days later, Herbie walked into the office, and with Bob close by, signed the recruitment papers. (Herbie was 19 and old enough to join the Marines without his guardians' consent. Bob, who was only 17, had to have his father approve his enlistment.) Since Herbie was supposed to graduate in 11 days, he figured he'd better call the Boys Town High School principal to tell him what he had done.

Herbie dialed the number and listened for a few seconds. Then he held the phone away from his ear.

"What's the matter, Herbie?" Bob asked.

"Mr. Crawford got mad and hung up on me," Herbie replied.

"Well," Bob said, "I guess now you have to join the Marines."

A short time later, the two young men boarded a train for San Diego, California. Each carried a suitcase and a youthful exuberance for adventure. Next stop: the United States Marine Corps.

The flare arced into the night sky over Bob Mitchell's company on Bunker Hill, then exploded with a soft pop, illuminating the hillside. Shrill bugles blared, and the air was torn by whining shells and the bright flash of tracer bullets.

A shell hit a forward foxhole, killing a young replacement Mitchell had gotten to know. The kid had just come up to the line and this was his first time in combat.

As hundreds of Chinese soldiers raced up the slope, rifle and machine-gun fire blazed from the Marines' trenches. A shell exploded behind Mitchell, blowing off his helmet and driving a piece of shrapnel into the back of his head. A young soldier who had been standing next to Mitchell — a kid from Nebraska — was killed by the blast.

Mitchell looked around for his helmet, momentarily dazed. He found it, put it on, then quickly put a battle dressing on his wound.

Now Mitchell's instincts and training took over. The Chinese charged up the hill and swept into the Marines' trenches. Savage hand-to-hand fighting raged up and down the line. The screams of men mingled with the din of gunfire and explosions. The battle became a fight for survival, with men using shovels, rifle butts, bayonets — any weapon they could lay their hands on. An enemy soldier charged Mitchell. Mitchell fired his pistol point-blank at the man. The soldier staggered a few steps toward him, then fell to the ground.

With their forward trenches overrun, the Marines began to pull back to their second line of defense on the other side of the hill. As the Chinese came over the top, they were cut down by a wall of lead as the Marine guns caught them out in the open. The few who were not killed or wounded stood on the hilltop, dazed and confused. Then they turned and ran.

The Chinese had thrown a reinforced battalion — more than 500 men — against the 250 Marines on the hill. Nearly half of the Marines were killed or wounded. But the Chinese did not take the hill.

The seriously wounded were carried to an emergency aid station. Mitchell spent three more days at the front before being relieved and sent to the rear for treatment of his wound.

"When they took me into the aid station, it was just like a meat-packing plant," Mitchell recalled. "They had these boards all the way down the tent — two rows of them. They had notches in them — that was for the stretchers. Then the doctors came in and took a look at me. They pulled most of the lead out of the back of my head. When the doctor dropped it in the basin, it was just like a rock hitting a piece of cement."

Some of the pieces were too small for the doctors to remove. Years later, Mitchell still would feel those tiny metal slivers.

Herbie Werner had never been so cold. The temperature had plummeted to 30 degrees below zero as he and the other Marines of his company tried to catch some sleep on the rock-hard ground.

It was December 1950. Werner was among the 15,000 Marines and United Nations troops who had been forced to retreat from the Chosin Reservoir when 130,000 Chinese Communist troops poured across the Yalu River to attack Allied forces.

The retreat turned into a torturous fight for survival.

Every day was the same. The deadly cold. The biting wind. The fatigue. The enemy.

The First Marine Division's column of soldiers and vehicles, loaded with the wounded and dead, crawled along the icy, twisting mountain roads. When the weather was good, Marine Corsairs dove in with air strikes against the enemy and artillery pounded their positions. Werner and his company had the dangerous job of protecting the column's flanks, fighting off the Chinese troops who constantly harassed and shelled the Marines.

When night fell, the column stopped. The Marines, bone-weary from the day's march, ate cold C rations. Werner and the other men always carried the food tins under their arms during the day; it was the only way to keep the food from freezing. Then they tried to warm their frostbitten feet in sleeping bags. Although every shivering Marine wanted to crawl inside his bag, they all knew it was dangerous to be stuck there if the enemy attacked.

The cold and exhaustion were terrible, but the waiting was worse. Behind hastily erected walls of snow and ice, haggard, bleary-eyed men tried to keep each other awake as they listened and watched.

Then it started. Whistles, bugles, shouts. Flares popped, illuminating the waves of screaming Chinese soldiers who were running toward the Marine positions. The sound of machine guns and rifles, wounded men crying out for their mothers, and the hollow thump of grenades merged to create a dull roar.

As the Chinese tumbled into the Marine lines, men grappled hand to hand. Some Marines swung shovels or rifles, fighting for their lives against three or four Chinese soldiers.

The battle swirled around Werner and his men as they fought to throw back the attack. Sometimes, the Chinese would fall back quickly. Other times, the Marines would slug it out with the enemy in an all-night firefight.

During lulls, medics helped the wounded and officers tried to reorganize the men who had become separated in the confusion of the fight.

When it got light, the wounded and the dead were loaded into trucks. Werner was assigned to a detail that picked up bodies for transport. Sometimes when the column had stopped, the detail piled bodies in a tent, leaving an aisle down the middle. All that was visible from the aisle were the boots of the dead.

During one search for bodies, Werner came upon the body of a British commando who had been shot in the head. The commando was wearing a good pair of cold-weather boots. Werner thought about his own frozen feet, then took the boots. He knew the commando wouldn't need them any more. That's just the way things were.

Werner kept telling himself they would make it out.

It was sometimes hard to remember what had happened so long ago. Before the Marines. Before Boys Town.

In 1930, when Herbie Werner was two years old, his mother gave him away. She placed an ad in a New York newspaper, asking for someone to take her son because she couldn't care for him anymore.

An older couple took him in and gave him a home. But they were poor. The couple moved to Newton, New Jersey, where they built a shack to live in. With the husband working most of the time just to put food on the table and the wife always sick, there was no one to provide guidance for Herbie or give him the attention he needed. And then there were the times when the husband would get angry and take it out on Herbie with a beating.

Herbie started staying away from home, wandering the streets with other boys. He got a job at a department store. One night, he and another boy stole some rifle ammunition and four tires from the store. They got caught and were placed on probation for one year.

Herbie's case caught the attention of a local priest. The priest believed that Herbie was a good boy; he just needed someone to show him the way. After talking to the judge who ordered the probation, the priest wrote a letter to Father Flanagan at Boys Town. He asked Father Flanagan to "accept this unruly boy not only for his own good but also for the common good of all concerned."

So at age 16, Herbie was put on a train for the five-day trip to Boys Town.

When the train arrived in Omaha, Herbie got off. But it was another two days before he worked up enough courage to go to Boys Town. He arrived there at night and was put up in Dormitory Four. The next day, the mayor gave him a tour of the campus and Herbie started meeting the other boys.

It wasn't long before Herbie started to feel at home at Boys Town. He joined the football and boxing teams, and became a member of the famed Boys Town Choir, which traveled all over the United States for performances. And he got to know Bob Mitchell and his older brother, Jim.

At the center of it all was Father Flanagan. Years later, Herbie would recall the way Father called everyone "dear."

"Even when he was punishing you, he'd say, 'Don't you ever do that again, dear,' and you wouldn't," Herbie said.

One of Herbie's most vivid memories of Father Flanagan

involved going to confession. He remembers that most of the boys tried to avoid the confessional they knew Father Flanagan was in.

"We did it because he'd hand out 500 'Hail Marys' and 100 'Our Fathers,'" Herbie said. "You'd end up with more sins than you started with."

Werner thought about those happy times as he marched on frozen feet through the wind-swept Korean mountains. "I had a real grand time there," he thought. He chuckled. "It'll be good to get back to Boys Town some day."

Bob Mitchell scraped the hard grease from the three small hamburger patties piled in the tin can. C rations. Old Faithful. Another cold meal and another cold night.

Mitchell had been in Korea since September 1950, when the Marines made the surprise landing at Inchon. He had seen plenty of fighting in the towns and villages as the Marines pushed inland and recaptured Seoul. But when the Chinese hit the Marines near the Chosin Reservoir, that's when he was most afraid.

It had been a week since the Marine retreat from the reservoir began. The Chinese, dressed in their bulky white uniforms and fur hats, had attacked on November 28. Confident of a quick victory over the outnumbered American, British, and South Korean units, the Chinese weren't prepared for long exposure to the 30-degree-below-zero temperatures. Many wore tennis shoes instead of boots and didn't carry extra clothing. When the Marines fought back and stopped the initial Chinese advance, hundreds of enemy soldiers froze to death in their positions on the mountain passes.

The Marines faced their own problems with the cold. Much of their gear was left over from World War II and included clothing better suited to the island campaigns in the Pacific. They had coats, but nothing heavy enough to stop the biting mountain winds. Like most of the Marines in the column, Mitchell tied strips of cloth around his shoes to try to keep his feet warm. It didn't help much. Most everyone had frostbite.

Lack of sleep plagued the Marines, too. Men leaned against trucks or Jeeps, or dozed on their feet whenever the column stopped. At night, there were fitful naps on the cold ground.

Mitchell, exhausted from lugging his 29-pound Browning automatic rifle, concentrated on following the man in front of him. It was about the only way to stay awake.

The Chinese were always there. During the day, at least, the Marine column got some help. Marine Corsairs bombed and napalmed enemy positions, and Allied artillery blasted away at troop concentrations. When the weather was good, C-47 cargo planes made air drops of ammunition, food, and other supplies.

Nighttime was different. The Chinese would attack any time, but they preferred the cover of darkness. It was always a big show before they hit. Lots of noise over loudspeakers. Then the flares would streak upward. After awhile, the Marines figured out a pattern in the flares and could guess when the attack would start.

The Marines huddled behind piles of snow or overturned trucks for cover. No one could dig a foxhole; the ground was frozen. And even when they knew the Chinese were coming, it was almost impossible to see them in their white outfits against the snow.

When that last flare went off, the Chinese were sometimes only 20 or 30 yards away. Then they would come in waves, yelling and screaming, and the Marines would fight them off.

Everyone was afraid. But no one gave up.

For 19-year-old Mitchell, the breakout was an ordeal of cold, death, and misery. During those grim days, Mitchell thought a lot about Boys Town and the friends he had made there. Guys like Jerry Howard and Jerry Kabeska and Leo Magers — other Boys Town kids who were fighting in Korea. He thought about what he had learned about toughness as a 5-foot-5, 123-pounder going up against a 200-pound giant on the football field. Discipline and strength and pride. And the sense of family and brotherhood he learned at Boys Town and in the Marine Corps. He knew survival hinged on depending on each other and having the will to survive.

Mitchell knew Herbie Werner was in the column somewhere. They'd seen each other just after the landings at Inchon, but then their outfits went different ways. Before that, the last time they'd been together was in August 1948. After three months in boot camp, they'd been sent to Camp Pendleton where Mitchell was assigned to an infantry battalion and Werner joined the regimental headquarters.

Good old Herbie, Mitchell thought. I hope he's okay.

Mitchell looked down at the cold hamburgers and slowly started eating.

On December 9, the final phase of the historic breakout from the Chosin Reservoir began. The First Marine Division advanced south to the key city of Koto-Ri, then fought its way out of the mountains and the enemy encirclement. Two weeks later, the division was in the North Korean port city of Hungnam where Navy ships were waiting to evacuate them.

Of the 13 men in his squad, only Herbie Werner and another man were still alive. As Werner's column of the division came out of the mountains, it brought with it three truckloads of dead Marines. Werner and nearly every man in his outfit suffered frostbitten fingers and toes.

The division suffered 718 dead, 192 missing, 3,485 wounded, and 7,338 nonbattle casualties.

But Marine pride and courage had turned what could have been a major defeat into an historic victory. Despite the odds against them, the Marines never gave up. In what would be hailed as one of the greatest achievements in Marine Corps history, the men of the Chosin Reservoir campaign decimated the Ninth Chinese Army Group, inflicting heavy casualties and slowing its advance south. Their holding action also allowed the Navy to evacuate nearly 100,000 North Korean refugees to safety. Survivors called it "The Christmas Miracle."

As they neared the harbor, the Marines and their British and South Korean comrades who had endured the march could see the Navy ships waiting for them. With Allied artillery still firing at enemy positions outside the city, they went on board, each man with a sense of relief and a sense of accomplishment.

Mitchell and Werner ended up on different ships. Neither man would know for several weeks that the other was okay. For now, being safe and warm was enough.

After what the Marines had been through, the ships were like palaces. Men peeled off filthy clothing they had worn for weeks. There were hot showers, hot food, and warm beds. They were able to shave and brush their teeth — all the little things they hadn't been able to do in the field.

The ships were crowded. The men had to eat in shifts, often standing up in the mess hall. They didn't mind; it sure beat standing on a frozen mountain road trying to scrape cold food from a can. And the soldiers didn't just eat; they gorged themselves. Werner would never forget watching a South Korean soldier dump half of bowl of sugar on a plate of spaghetti before hungrily devouring the sweetened pasta.

As the evacuation fleet sailed south through the Sea of Japan, the bustle of getting clean and fed and finding a place to sleep gradually gave way to quiet. There were no explosions or gunfire now. No wounded men crying out. No screaming shells or bugles. As they lay on their bunks or smoked a last cigarette before going to sleep, Mitchell and Werner and hundreds of others wondered how and why they had made it. They thought about friends who were killed or wounded, and grieved for them. And they thought about home.

As the weary soldiers slept, the only sound was the steady drone of the ship's engines.

The images of the march from the Chosin Reservoir stayed with Bob Mitchell. He would never forget the miserable cold and the fierce fighting. Or having to push stalled vehicles off the road, or burning weapons so they wouldn't fall into enemy hands. And the haggard faces of young men whose sunken eyes and hollowed cheeks made them look so much older.

Mitchell later would learn that a Marine named Hector Caparota, a buddy from boot camp, received the Congressional Medal of Honor. Caparota, who was with another unit during the breakout, had taken his boots off and put his feet in a sleeping bag to warm them. The Chinese hit during the night and Caparota grabbed his automatic rifle and fought through the night, barefoot. His actions saved the company, but Caparota's legs froze and both had to be amputated above the knee.

Herbie Werner thought about what he had just been through, too. He remembered how eager he and his buddies had been to get to Korea when their orders came in. They called themselves "hot to trot."

"Everybody was enthusiastic and couldn't wait to get with the program. We knew what we had to do. We were trained for it. We just wanted to get over there and do the job," Werner would recall later. "When we got there, it was a different story. None of us had ever seen dead bodies."

Werner had landed at Pusan in August 1950, part of the first group of Marines sent to Korea.

A semicircle of defensive positions, known as the Pusan Perimeter, had been established around the port city after the initial North Korean attack on the south. Werner was in a truck convoy on the perimeter when he got his first taste of combat.

"We were getting shelled on the road and in a riverbed area. I remember going into a hole that was just big enough for one person. There was another Marine there and we both squeezed in."

When the shelling ended, seven Marines were dead. A woman who had been directing artillery fire on the Marines was captured and executed by a South Korean soldier.

While on the Pusan Perimeter, Werner saw plenty of frontline action serving as a messenger for a colonel. He suffered a gunshot wound to the leg during a firefight but was back with his unit in four days. A few months later, he was aboard a ship, waiting to go ashore at Inchon.

Then came the retreat from the reservoir.

Now, safe and warm on the evacuation ship, Werner could still see the faces of wounded men. The men were lying in straw that covered the floor of an old house that had been set up as a medical aid station. Even in the dim light of the lanterns, he could see the pain in their eyes.

Bob Mitchell's ship sailed to the South Korean port city of Masan after the evacuation. His company spent a couple of weeks in a rear area, resting and reorganizing. Then it was ordered back to the front lines.

Two months later, on March 17, 1951, Mitchell was hit during a firefight in the town of Munsanee. A machine-gun bullet shattered a bone in his left leg. He was taken to a forward aid station, then evacuated to a hospital ship. Weeks later, he was in a military hospital in Oakland, California, where doctors operated and saved the leg.

Recovery was a slow process. Mitchell spent nearly four months in the hospital before he was well enough to return to duty. Then he was assigned to Camp Pendleton in San Diego, where he trained troops who were getting ready to go to Korea.

Mitchell was awarded the Purple Heart for his wound. His first tour of duty was behind him.

Herbie Werner's ship also docked at Masan following the

evacuation voyage. His unit rested, then returned to front-line duty for several months. In April 1951, Werner shipped out to Japan, where he boarded a troop ship bound for the United States.

As the ship passed under the Golden Gate Bridge in San Francisco Bay a few weeks later, a Navy band welcomed the Marines home. Thirty wounded men were taken off the ship as Marines scrambled around the dock looking for their friends.

Werner and his buddies spotted a table where milk was being served. Not having tasted fresh milk for months, the Marines drank glass after glass, until they couldn't hold any more.

Werner spent his first few days back in the States with a terrible stomachache.

Graduation Day, 1951.

The members of Boys Town's senior class filed into the auditorium and took their seats. On the stage sat Monsignor Nicholas Wegner, executive director of Boys Town since Father Flanagan's death in 1948. Other dignitaries included Omaha Archbishop Gerald T. Bergan and actor Pat O'Brien, who had been invited to speak at the ceremony.

There was another special guest in the auditorium that July day. He waited patiently as the graduates crossed the stage one by one to receive their diplomas from Monsignor Wegner.

Then 23-year-old Sgt. Herbie Werner, wearing the Marine uniform he left Boys Town for three years earlier, stepped forward. The diploma he had missed by 11 days when he joined the Marines in 1948 was handed to him, and a smile spread across his face. He was a Boys Town graduate.

In June 1952, Bob Mitchell volunteered for a second tour of duty in Korea. He had made up his mind to make a career of the Marine Corps and figured a Marine should do the job he was trained for.

"It was harder than hell, if you were an instructor or a troop handler, to train these people to go somewhere and see them leave and not go with them," Mitchell would say later.

By the time Mitchell got back to the war in July 1952, it had turned into defensive stalemate. Both sides tried to hold the ground they had captured while negotiators in Panmunjom tried to hammer out a peace plan. This didn't mean an end to the bloodshed. The United Nations forces and the Chinese continued to launch attacks, hoping to gain a battleground advantage that could be used as a bargaining chip at the peace talks.

Mitchell's company became part of the tug of war being played out on the battlefield. Send out patrols. Assess the enemy's strength. Push the Chinese off a hill. Move out and let the Chinese move back in.

It was during these operations that Mitchell's company fought off the Chinese attack on Bunker Hill. Mitchell spent 30 days in a rear area after being wounded in the battle, then returned to his unit at the front.

In early spring 1953, he received orders to report for duty in Japan. He flew out of Inchon to a Marine camp in Kyoto and, to his surprise, found out that he was going to play baseball for the Marine Corps service team in the Far East. The officers in charge of the team had gone through the records of Marines who were being rotated back to the States looking for players. Mitchell, who had been an excellent outfielder at Boys Town, was picked for the team.

Mitchell's team was on its way to winning the Far East championship when the fighting in Korea ended on July 27, 1953.

Herbie Werner looked down from his outpost on the village of Panmunjom. Truce negotiations had started there in October 1951 and had been going on with little progress for nearly two years.

Werner, now a staff sergeant, was in charge of a 4.2-inch mortar platoon. His outfit had seen major action defending a series of outposts near the 38th parallel, the no-man's-land between the Chinese and United Nations forces.

This was Werner's second tour of duty in Korea. He had re-enlisted in 1952, when his first hitch ended, deciding to make the Marine Corps his career. In August, he volunteered to return to Korea. Although trench warfare now dominated the conflict, there had been several big battles in which his platoon had provided support fire.

It was now July 27, 1953. A day like any other day. Breakfast. Clean weapons. Orders for the day.

Then the message that everyone wanted to hear: The negotiators had signed an armistice. If the truce held, the war was over.

Werner and his men welcomed the news with relief and joy. But there wasn't much time to celebrate. Werner's platoon was ordered to guard a bridge that would be used for an exchange of prisoners. He and his men watched as a convoy of trucks carrying North Korean prisoners came down the road to the bridge. As the trucks approached the bridge, the prisoners screamed and yelled, cursing the Marines as they passed. A steady rain of clothing and shoes that had been issued to the prisoners when they were captured flew out of the trucks as the men disdainfully stripped off their captors' garments.

Everyone was happy to be going home.

Mitchell and Werner both returned to the United States in spring 1954. Bob had two Purple Hearts; Herbie was awarded a Purple Heart and the Navy Commendation Medal with a Combat V.

The years that followed brought a number of different assignments for both men. Werner got married in 1954; Mitchell was married in 1951 while on leave from duty in Korea. With their careers and families, it became harder to stay in touch with each other.

Mitchell spent several years at various bases in Japan and the Far East. In 1961, he was sent to Vietnam where he served three and a half months as an advisor to the South Vietnamese Army. He went back to Vietnam in 1965. During a 13-month tour, he was wounded three times and earned the Silver Star for leading the survivors of a patrol that had been ambushed back to safety.

In 1968, after 20 years in the Corps, Mitchell retired. As fate would have it, Boys Town again entered his life.

"I had an appointment in Omaha to get a job at the Post Office," he would recall later. "I was supposed to go down there on Monday. I showed up in Nebraska on the Friday before my appointment. This is August 1968.

"The first place I went was my brother Charlie's house. Charlie ran the Print Shop at Boys Town. I went out to Boys Town with him the next day. I said, 'Are you the only one in here?'

"Charlie just said, 'Forget the Post Office. Why don't you go up and ask Father Wegner if you can come down here and work for me?'

"I didn't know Father Wegner but Charlie took me and introduced me to him. I went to work in the Print Shop Aug. 22, 1968."

One more surprise awaited Mitchell.

Mitchell had passed his high school equivalency test while he was in the Marines but had never received a diploma. Shortly after he began working at Boys Town, one of his old coaches, Mitt Stoffel, gave Bob his high school diploma from Boys Town. It was dated 1949: the year he would have graduated.

Werner also served two tours of duty in Vietnam, in 1968 and 1969. He was wounded twice (once spending several weeks in a military hospital on Guam after being hit in the knee and foot by shrapnel), and received the Silver Star and the Bronze Star.

After Vietnam, Werner moved up through the ranks and received command and training assignments at Camp Pendleton and Parris Island in the United States, and at bases in Europe and in the Far East.

In 1985, with 37 years of active service behind him, Major Herbert Werner retired from the Marine Corps.

Summer 1983.

Herbie Werner wheeled his car into the main entrance of the Boys Town campus. The place had changed a lot since he last visited 30 years earlier.

He had been looking forward to this reunion for a long time. Many years had passed since he and Bob Mitchell had seen each other. And other old friends would be there, too. They were all coming back to the place they called home.

As soon as Herbie got out of the car, the tears came. Bob was waiting for him. The two friends who had taken that first big step toward manhood together shook hands, then embraced.

It was good to be home again.

Bob Mitchell continues to work at the Boys Town Print Shop where he is the Lead Print Production Supervisor. He and his wife, Marjorie, live in Omaha. Their three sons served in the military — one in the Marines and two in the Army — and one saw action in Operation Desert Storm. One of the couple's two daughters is married to a serviceman.

Herbert Werner has worked for the California State Prison System since early 1986. At the time of publication, he was the assistant superintendent in prison industry at Richard J. Dawson Prison in San Diego. Werner and his wife, Mary, live in Chula Vista, California. They have one daughter.

★ six ★

Flight of the orphans

Song Yong Cho sat up in bed. On both sides of him boys were sleeping peacefully in beds just like his. For a moment, he forgot where he was. Were the shells coming? Should he hide? Why didn't his stomach hurt from hunger? Then he remembered. He was safe. He was in America. He was at Boys Town.

Song's nightmares were understandable. He had survived an ordeal that had almost cost him his life. But he was one of the lucky ones. For every South Korean child like Song who was rescued, there were thousands who perished.

A lot had happened since Song came to America. But it was hard to forget what life had been like before.

Eight-year-old Song and his family had been living near the South Korean capital of Seoul when the North Koreans attacked in June 1950. Over the next few months, the family sought safety wherever it could, trying to avoid capture by enemy patrols that were rounding up the city's inhabitants.

On September 15, United Nations forces led by U.S. Marines and Army troops landed at the port city of Inchon, west of Seoul. Within two weeks, they had retaken the capital and driven out the North Koreans.

But in December, Seoul again became a target for invaders from the north. This time Chinese troops that had crossed their border to attack U.N. forces were advancing toward the city, and residents began fleeing to the safety of areas still under American or South Korean control. Amid the chaos of the evacuation, Song was separated from his family.

With no one to care for him and no place to go, Song joined the mass exodus of refugees who were fleeing the war-torn city. Song eventually fell in with a group that was headed for Pusan, about 225 miles away.

The journey was miserable. The harsh Korean winter brought biting winds, blinding snow, and unbearable cold. The bedraggled refugees never had enough to eat and many became sick. Song, who didn't have any shoes or warm clothing, trudged down snow-covered roads, struggling to keep up with the others. With little protection from the cold, it was only a short time before the youngster's bare feet became severely frostbitten. The frozen flesh soon turned black and gangrene set in. No longer able to walk, Song laid down along the road halfway to Pusan as the stream of refugees flowed by.

It was then that the first of Song's "guardian angels" appeared. A woman who lived along the road found the sick boy, carried him to her home, and fed him. Then the woman's son, a South Korean army captain, took Song to a makeshift hospital. Song would live but it was too late to save his feet. Doctors amputated both of them and part of each leg below the knee.

"Everyone was nice and kind, but I was afraid about my feet," Song would tell people later. "Then the doctors took my legs away. It hurt."

Because the hospital was so overcrowded with sick and wounded, Song was evacuated to an orphanage in Pusan. Like most of the other children there, he didn't like the place. Soon, despite his disability, he left to roam the streets.

To support himself, Song made a wooden shoeshine box and began shining the boots of American soldiers at a railroad station in Pusan. Every day, soldiers waiting for their train would watch as the boy with the big grin dragged himself across the muddy ground on his buttocks, the box hanging around his neck. At night, when there were no more customers, Song took the little money he had earned, bought a meager meal, then settled into a doorway or alley for the night.

The months passed. Then in April 1952, a second guardian angel came into Song's life.

The night Sgt. Harold Douglas's army troop ship arrived in Pusan Harbor was lousy — windy, cold, and wet. After disembarking from the ship, Douglas and his comrades headed for the railway station where they would board a troop train.

Then the soldiers saw them. Dozens of children, each carrying a shoeshine box, running toward them. The kids had heard the troop ship whistle in the harbor and knew that it meant there would be many boots to shine. The boots of paying customers.

As Douglas surveyed the horde of young entrepreneurs, his eyes stopped on one dirty little boy in ragged clothes. The youngster was trying his best to keep up with the others, but was having trouble as he half-crawled, half-hopped down the slushy street. Then Douglas saw that the boy had no feet. At the end of filthy trouser legs were squares of rubber that the youngster had tied on to protect his stumps.

Douglas, who had seven children of his own back home in Hattiesburg, Mississippi, felt a catch in his throat. He beckoned the boy over and lifted his boot. The kid smiled and went to work.

Despite the cold, the grin never left the boy's face. Douglas thought about his own children and wondered how this little guy had survived. A few minutes later, a train whistle screeched, and the soldiers headed for the boarding area. Douglas gave the dark-haired boy a last look and tossed him a half dollar. Song grinned as the GI trotted away.

All the way to his camp, Douglas thought about the little boy with no feet. With no one to take care of him and with his disability, it was unlikely that he'd survive much longer.

As soon as Douglas got settled in, he returned to Pusan with a buddy who spoke Korean and again found the boy. Over a hot meal, Song told his story to the sergeant through the interpreter. Song said he'd never been to school, so he didn't know how to read or write. As they talked, Douglas noticed that Song's body was covered with sores and welts. He decided then that he couldn't let the boy go back to his life on the street.

When Douglas and his buddy got back on the train that day, Song was with them.

Douglas received permission from his commanding officer to house Song in the enlisted men's quarters. Song took his first shower, and Douglas cleaned and put medicine on the boy's sores. Song got clean clothes and a warm bed. And best of all, there was plenty of food.

Song quickly became a favorite of the GIs in Douglas's unit. They taught him simple English phrases and showed him how to play baseball. One day, Douglas and some of the other men gave Song a present. The boy eagerly ripped open the package. There, inside, was a shiny new pair of army boots. Song smiled, then glanced down at his half-empty pant legs. How could he wear these wonderful new boots?

Douglas smiled. "You'll be able to wear those boots soon enough," he said. Then he told the boy that he was working on getting him two new feet — artificial feet. Douglas had already contacted Capt. James Calway, commanding officer of the First Artificial Limb and Brace detachment of the 14th Field Hospital near Pusan, about having the boy fitted with prosthetic feet.

A short time later, Sgt. Richard Gormanson designed the artificial feet for Song and began teaching him how to walk.

Song practiced on the new limbs every day, at first using crutches. Then the day came when he laced up his new boots, threw the crutches aside, and walked. As the grinning kid awkwardly hobbled across a roomful of soldiers, tears mixed with smiles.

So now Song could walk, Douglas thought. But what happens when the war ends and we all leave? Song would be back on the streets again. The ideal situation was for Douglas to adopt Song and take him home to the United States. But with seven children already, Douglas didn't think that was a practical solution. No, there had to be something more he could do.

Then an idea came to him. Boys Town.

Douglas had heard about the village in Nebraska and how it welcomed orphaned or abandoned boys. Song wasn't an American orphan but he was still an orphan. It was a long shot but if it meant helping Song find a better life in America, it was worth a try.

The first letters to Monsignor Nicholas Wegner, Boys Town's executive director, were written by Capt. Calway and Douglas in October 1952. After explaining Song's situation and how he came to be in an American army camp, Calway wrote:

> Our job here may be completed after the first of the year and then we will move on. It would seem inhuman to have this boy return to the environment from which we took him. Due to the conditions, confusion and uncertainty existing here in Korea, I would not feel secure concerning his care and welfare, now and in the future, by placing him in an institution in this country. He has not had any type of schooling and cannot read and write. It would be ideal if he could learn a vocation at Boys Town. Due to his age, disability and lack of parents, he will need care and guid-

ance until he is old enough to care for himself.

I have spoken to Monsignor Carroll (company chaplain) and introduced him to this boy and we both feel that his case presents extenuating circumstances which you through your generosity could solve.

Therefore I am appealing to you to use your influence in trying to place this child in Boys Town in the States.

Douglas told Wegner:

The boy has shown that he is intelligent, energetic and capable of being rehabilitated. He has a wonderful personality and all who have come in contact with him have been attracted to him.

Being the father of seven children, it is impossible for me to consider adoption of this boy, but I would gladly do so if I did not have such a large family already.

Captain Calway has been wonderful to the boy and is truly a fine and sincere man. His request for Song's acceptance into Father Flanagan's Boys' Home was a very considerate and Christian gesture and I sincerely hope that it can be accomplished.

Thank you, Father, for your interest in this little boy.

Two weeks later, Monsignor Wegner replied to the men, telling them he would do everything he could to admit Song to Boys Town. He cautioned, however, that strict immigration laws would make it difficult for Song to enter the United States. Wegner told Calway and Douglas that if they could get other officers to send him letters of support for Song, it would give him more clout when he contacted friends in the U.S. Senate about introducing a special bill to allow Song to enter the country.

Soon Wegner was flooded with messages from high-ranking officers who knew of Song and who wanted to help him get to Boys Town.

Wegner then contacted two acquaintances — U.S. Sen. Hugh Butler and U.S. Rep. Roman Hruska — for assistance. The two congressmen from Nebraska introduced special bills to allow Song to come to the United States. Wegner even went to Washington to plead Song's case before the Senate Committee on Immigration. After several delays, legislation that established quotas for Asians was approved. Song would be the first Korean orphan to benefit from the new law.

When the news that Song was going to Boys Town hit Pusan, it set off a flurry of activity. Servicemen, nurses, and others who knew Song contributed $400 for his air fare to the States. There were also donations of clothing Song would need; Maryknoll missionary nuns even had a new suit made for the youngster.

Finally, on May 22, 1953, Song took his first steps toward America as he walked toward a Northwest Airlines plane at Pusan Airport. Wearing a green cowboy hat, a green shirt, and denim pants, Song was hugged by well-wishers who pressed dollar bills into his hand as he boarded the plane. Then he was gone, enroute to his new home. (Ironically, the war that had taken his family and his feet from him would end a few weeks later.)

Stewardesses watched out for the boy during the long trans-Pacific flight. Song, who was understandably shy around strangers, didn't have any meals, but snacked on chocolate bars and glasses of milk.

Song first flew to Seattle, Washington, where he was greeted by the wife of Richard Gormanson, the serviceman who had designed Song's first pair of artificial feet. There also was a mob of photographers and reporters. Unknown to Song, his trip to America had become big news, and newspapers and magazines all across the country followed his every move once he was in the United States. As flashbulbs popped and reporters shouted questions, Song just flashed his winning grin and nodded happily. From Seattle, Song flew to Minneapolis, where Monsignor Wegner was waiting for him. They completed the final leg of Song's journey to Boys Town together.

It was late when Song's plane touched down in Omaha. During the car ride from the airport, a travel-weary Song dozed next to Monsignor Wegner. As they approached Boys Town, Song looked out the window. Even through the darkness, he could make out the big trees, the rolling hills, and the neat brick buildings of the sleeping "City of Little Men." It looked so peaceful. And it felt different. It felt safe. There were no jets streaking overhead or booming artillery. The air smelled fresh and clean, not smoky like back in Korea. There was no war here.

Still, Song was worried and scared. Here he was, a stranger from another country. He didn't speak English, and didn't know a lot about American customs. He was far away from the soldiers who had been his friends. He looked different and he didn't have real feet like all the other boys. This was a new world and he was afraid. Would the other boys want him to stay? Would they accept him? And most importantly, would they like him?

Song drifted off to sleep that night thinking about everything that had happened to him. He hoped he had found a good home.

The next morning, Song got an answer to at least some of his questions about being accepted. As he awoke, he felt something under his pillow. He lifted the pillow and there were two shiny toy six-shooters and a holster, just like American cowboys carried. Two boys had left the toys during the night, a gift that said, "Welcome, brother. You're one of us."

Later, Song was introduced to the 800 other boys who would be his new family. More gifts were presented — comic books, toys, baseballs, games. Boys Town Mayor Bill Maddux gave Song a shoeshine. Monsignor Wegner gave Song a watch. Photographers took more pictures and reporters asked more questions. Song even got to sit in Monsignor Wegner's big office chair. Overwhelmed by all the attention, Song said little. But the smile was there, growing even wider when Wegner would say, "Chi sai," a Japanese phrase that means "smiling little boy."

As the weeks and months passed, Song became more accustomed to his new surroundings. He began to learn English from a Korean tutor, and was enrolled in school. Despite his disability, Song played baseball and swam (he would remove his artificial feet and the other boys would throw him in the lake). He could beat just about anybody at checkers, a game he learned from GIs in Korea. And he loved to watch television, especially shoot-'em-up Westerns.

When it came to eating, Song was in heaven. His favorite foods were hot dogs with mustard, fried chicken, watermelon, and vanilla ice cream.

Song also became somewhat of a national celebrity. The public's interest in the small Korean orphan continued as Song appeared on television programs and made appearances with Monsignor Wegner. His life in Korea and at Boys Town also was the subject of dozens of magazine and newspaper articles.

On one trip, Song traveled with Wegner to New York City to call attention to the plight of Korean war orphans. The boy met the mayor and attended Mass at St. Patrick's Cathedral. Before Mass, Richard Cardinal Spellman, the Archbishop of New York, asked that Song be brought to his residence so the archbishop could meet the boy. When Spellman entered the room, Monsignor Wegner knelt on one knee and kissed the archbishop's ring. As Song struggled to kneel, Spellman grasped the boy's elbows, lifted him up, then knelt down himself. "We learn from the courage of children, too," Spellman said.

During his years at Boys Town, Song received hundreds of letters and gifts from well-wishers, and at least one family offered him a place to live when he graduated. Even after he left Boys Town, Song continued to receive letters and gifts from people. One college girl wrote to tell him that her sorority would give him a new set of prostheses, donated by her father's artificial limb business.

School was tough for Song, mainly because he had received no formal schooling before coming to Boys Town. As for his English, he had picked up some phrases from the soldiers he lived with in Korea, and they had read him books and tried to teach him some basic English. But Song's vocabulary was limited.

A misunderstanding about Song's capabilities hampered his progress even more. When Song first arrived at Boys Town, his Korean tutor asked him whether he could do fourth-grade work. To Song, the word "work" meant physical labor, so he answered yes.

"You know, I never did tell them I couldn't do the school work," Song would recall years later. "All I did was sit in the classroom all year."

But as Song's English improved, so did his school work. He made the honor roll as a freshman. He struggled somewhat in high school, but continued to work hard. He knew that having a good education was an important part of American life.

"Over there (Korea) you can't go to school no matter how hard you want to," Song said once in an interview. "When you get big, there is no job. Most times you beg on a corner or go hungry. Here they tell me there will be a job. I will study hard and I will be ready."

Baptized a Catholic while in Korea, Song became an altar boy and received the Ad Altare Dei Award for serving Mass. He joined the Boy Scouts, eventually earning 21 merit badges and the coveted Eagle Scout award, scouting's highest honor. He played the drum in the Boys Town High School marching band. Despite his disability, he became an accomplished swimmer and lifeguard, and competed in intramural sports. He also served as Boys Town's first student athletic trainer.

Song was well-liked and well-respected by the other boys. They would often chant, "Let's go, Song!" as he gloved ground balls on the baseball field. He was seldom self-conscious about his feet and had little trouble keeping up with the other kids. A slight limp was the only hint of his handicap.

While he was always busy with school, sports, and other activities, Song never was too busy to stay in touch with the people who had made his new life possible. He often wrote letters to Harold Douglas, who returned home to teach at Southern Mississippi College, and to Richard Gormanson, who stayed in the prosthesis business after leaving the Army. In 1955, Song vacationed at Douglas's home in Mississippi and visited again in 1957 and 1958 when he attended Boy Scout camps in the state.

On Nov. 25, 1959, Song legally changed his name to honor his two best friends — Harold Douglas and Richard Gormanson. Four months later, 19-year-old Richard Douglas Cho became a citizen of the United States.

An American citizen! Eight years earlier, in the muddy streets of Pusan, he didn't even know where America was. Now he was part of the country where anything was possible.

But what would he do with this gift? In just a few months, he would be leaving Boys Town. For the past seven years, he had been part of the only family he could remember. He had found happiness and love at Boys Town, and he had grown from a helpless child to a capable man. Where would he go when he left Boys Town? How would he take care of himself without the people who had changed his life so much?

Those questions were on Richard's mind as he sat in a crowded auditorium in June 1960. Then, his name was called, and he rose and walked toward Monsignor Wegner. The priest smiled, hugged Richard, and handed him a diploma. The smile that had endeared Richard to so many when he was a boy now lit up the young man's face.

A short time later, Cho moved into an apartment near downtown Omaha. With Boys Town's help, he enrolled in a business college and began classes in clerical work.

Cho, however, still wasn't sure what he wanted to do with his life. After his graduation from the business college, he traveled to Arizona with friends, then went to Kansas City to visit a couple who had befriended him during a summer vacation when he was at Boys Town. Cho decided to stay in Kansas City and moved in with the couple. He eventually got a job as a bookkeeper at a pipe and steel company and moved into his own apartment.

Cho continued to rely on Boys Town for support and, from time to time, financial help. In his letters to Monsignor Wegner, he always talked about how much Boys Town had done for him.

In September 1961, he wrote to Wegner:

> I don't have to tell you how grateful I am for all the help I have received from you during my stay at Boys Town. All the boys have learned well because we had the best teachers and the best of everything. During our residence at the home, you and your staff consistently gave advice to us and now it has taken effect not only in our work but in our daily lives.
>
> If it wasn't for you, I don't know where or what I would be doing in my native country.

Cho moved several more times during the next few years, and on occasion visited Boys Town. Eventually, he decided to settle in Hawaii and found work as an accountant.

Cho long ago gave up any interest in returning to Korea; he conceded that a search for his family or other relatives would be fruitless.

And the pain of childhood and the confusion of trying to

start over in a new country long ago gave way to contentment. Just as when he was a small boy learning to walk on his first set of artificial feet, his next step is much more important than the last one.

★   ★   ★

The first time he saw the magazine pictures, Shu Che Hu knew that America was a special, magical place. There were cars and homes, telephones and cameras, upholstered chairs and beds. There was even sliced bread wrapped in cellophane. And the people in the pictures all looked happy and content.

The American soldiers who had taken him in had given him the magazines. He would sit and listen to the soldiers for hours as they talked about their homes. To a poor 10-year-old Korean boy, it seemed that every one of them had a nice house, a car, plenty of food and clothing, and money to buy other things, just like in the magazines.

Shu wondered how life could be so different in another land. Because for as long as he could remember, he had known only poverty, disease, hunger, and war.

Shu had been living with his family near Seoul when the North Koreans attacked in June 1950. Separated from his parents in the fighting, the boy was placed in an orphanage run by a stern old woman. Forty other boys lived in the one-room building, each night sleeping on the floor and each day working in a garden. The vegetables they raised were sold for money that was used to buy food and other necessities.

One day, as air raid sirens wailed, a bomb blasted the orphanage building. The boys scattered, eventually joining the flood of refugees trying to make their way out of the city. With North Korean forces advancing from the north, Shu and the other children headed south, hoping to cross the Han River to safety.

But the only bridge across the river had been destroyed. Shu and three other boys became separated from the other children, and not knowing where to go, returned to the orphanage. After wandering about the city for several days, scrounging food and avoiding enemy soldiers, the boys headed south.

Near Taejon, they happened on an American Army unit. A mess sergeant invited the rag-tag group into the mess hall for a meal. That night, the sergeant found a warm place where the boys could bed down. For the first time in weeks, Shu and his friends had full bellies and a good night's sleep.

Life around the Army camp was exciting for Shu. There was always lots of activity – trucks, tanks, infantrymen all preparing for action at the front. Best of all, there were three meals every day. Soon, Shu was helping in the mess hall, peeling potatoes, washing dishes, and mopping floors. When the unit moved out, heading north, Shu went along.

Shu continued to work in the mess hall and started to receive a little money, in addition to his meals and a place to sleep. Because the GIs had trouble pronouncing his name, they started calling Shu "Little Joe." As they got to know him better, the soldiers let Shu wander around the barracks and spend time in the day room, where the soldiers went to relax or write letters. It was in the day room that Shu started learning about the American way of life from the soldiers and the magazines.

Eventually, Shu began to wonder, "Why couldn't I go to America? Why can't I have these things?"

Shu knew that the soldiers wouldn't be around forever. Someday, they would leave and he would be left behind. There was nothing for him in Korea except more misery. Shu had to get to America. But how?

Cautiously, the boy began to question the GIs, trying to find out more about this wondrous country. He also began to save his money; he knew he would need it. At this point, Shu wasn't even sure where America was. But it didn't matter; he was going there.

Now fate turned against the boy. While riding on a South Korean army truck with several soldiers, Shu suffered a deep gash to his leg when the vehicle overturned. He spent two weeks in a Korean hospital, a stay that cost him his entire $28 in savings.

Heartbroken, Shu returned to the Army mess hall and started back to work. About this time, he met an older Korean man who was working at the post as an interpreter. They became friends and Shu told the man that he was planning to go to America.

Not wanting the boy to be disappointed, the interpreter carefully explained that America was on the other side of the world. There was no way to get there except by boat from Japan.

Then he would walk to Japan, the boy insisted.

No, the man told him. The only way was to get on a ship in Pusan and sail to Japan. But even if Shu got to Pusan, the man said, he would have to have a reason to go to Japan, a reason the Americans would believe.

Wanting to help Shu, the interpreter then came up with a story for the boy to use. Shu would tell the authorities in Pusan that he was Japanese and that his parents had been killed in bombing raids during World War II. American troops had adopted him in Japan and brought him to Korea with them when they were shipped to Korea. Now he was trying to get back to Fukuoka, a city in Japan, to search for his relatives there.

A few days later, Shu set out for Pusan, 200 miles away. As he walked along the road, he rehearsed his story, getting each detail down in his mind. Walking and hitching rides, Shu covered about 35 miles in three days. Then one morning, after spending the night in an abandoned farmhouse, he heard a most extraordinary noise.

He ran outside and looked up as four jets roared overhead, followed by four more of the sleek planes. One by one, the aircraft peeled out of their formation and slowly descended, disappearing behind some trees just before they touched down on the ground.

Shu didn't know much about jets but he knew from watching them that they traveled fast. If he could get a ride on one of those jets, he could be in Japan in no time. Walking toward the place where the aircraft had landed, he realized that he had stumbled onto a U.S. Air Force base. Shu hurriedly found the front gate and started inside.

But Air Force bases in a war zone did not welcome visitors, especially Korean boys who could be communist spies. The Air Police placed Shu under arrest and began questioning him.

Carefully, Shu recited the story he and the old man had concocted. He finished by asking if there was any work he could do on the base.

The police listened to the story. They knew thousands of Japanese and Korean families had been torn apart by the war. This story sounded plausible, and they felt sorry for the kid. Satisfied that he wasn't a spy, the police issued an identity card so Shu could look for work on the base, then released him.

With his experience, Shu quickly landed a job in the air base mess hall. He soon endeared himself to the pilots and other Air Force personnel, who would playfully tease and joke with the dark-haired boy at mealtime.

Shu enjoyed the attention and having a place to live. But he was no closer to Japan, or America, than he was when he started. Worse, Shu had learned that it was not easy to get a ride on an airplane to Japan. A person had to have orders or the permission of a high-ranking officer. Shu had neither. All he could do was watch as planes took off and disappeared into the eastern sky. As the spring of 1952 started, Shu's dream of reaching the United States appeared to be fading.

Then, a miracle.

A colonel at the base who heard Shu's story decided he might be able to do something for the boy. Although the regulations strictly forbade civilians from traveling on the daily courier flights to Japan, the colonel believed that this case allowed for some flexibility. One day, the colonel walked into the mess hall where Shu was working and asked the boy if he still wanted to go to Japan.

Surprised, Shu answered, "Yes sir."

"Get your things together," the officer said. "You're on your way."

A half hour later, Shu was aboard a C-46 cargo plane headed for Itazuke Air Base in Fukuoka, Japan.

The flight officers at the air base were surprised when a little boy climbed off the big airplane. This was not regulation. He would definitely have to go back on the next plane. But after learning that the boy had been put on the plane by a colonel in Korea, the officers reconsidered. This was a matter for the Air Police, they figured, and had Shu taken to headquarters. There, a kind but puzzled lieutenant colonel called the base chaplain, Father (1st Lt.) Donald Werr, for help.

The priest listened intently as Shu told his story. When Werr asked questions about where the boy's relatives might be, Shu was vague and uncertain. The priest felt something about the story just didn't sound right. But for now, the main thing was to find a place for the boy to stay. And since Shu was so eager to work, Werr agreed to help him get a job on the base. The priest called Marge Binder, a service club hostess, who said the boy could work at the club as a janitor.

For the next few weeks, Shu swept the floor and emptied waste baskets at the service club and shined shoes at the officers' club. He went about his work quietly and didn't talk much. Werr occasionally stopped by to check on the boy, brought him ice cream, and took him to the movies. Although he was having some doubts about the boy's story — Shu didn't have the typical Japanese features and now was evasive when the subject of his relatives came up — the priest wanted to help and did what he could to make him comfortable.

As the weeks passed, Shu began to change. He became less

shy and more friendly. The different units on the base started to go out of their way to do nice things for him. Members of the Air Police wrote home for warm clothing and shoes for the boy. The men in the communications unit gave him a small radio to wear on his wrist. And Miss Binder, the hostess at the social club, became Shu's unofficial guardian, helping him learn more English words and making sure he tended to things like brushing his teeth and showering.

As Werr got to know Shu better, he saw that the boy was intelligent, eager to learn, and cheerful. One day, Werr asked Shu if he wanted to learn to read and write English. Shu excitedly accepted the offer. Werr used military manuals and pamphlets as textbooks and Shu threw himself into his studies.

The bond between boy and priest was cemented for good during one particular study session. The word "family" came up and Shu asked Werr what it meant. The chaplain explained that it referred to a person's mother and father, sisters and brothers.

Shu asked Werr if he had a family. Werr told the boy that he had two sisters but no brothers.

"I could be your brother, maybe," Shu asked in a hopeful voice.

"Sure," Werr said, smiling. "You're my little brother from now on."

From that time on, Shu felt he had someone he could depend on, someone who would take care of him. It was almost like having a family.

Shu hadn't mentioned his desire to get to America to Werr and he still wasn't sure how he was going to get there. He decided that while he was waiting, he would at least act as American as he could. So he asked Werr to give him a name, a name with two parts, like all Americans had. Besides, he had been called "Little Joe" ever since he had latched on with the army. He felt grown up now and he didn't want to be called "little" anymore.

Werr didn't have to think long. Joseph was a good first

name. And what better name than "Anthony" for someone in this child's predicament. Anthony, as in the patron saint of lost objects. Joseph later would be baptized a Catholic under his new name.

Through the summer of 1952, Joseph continued to work hard on his studies. Werr soon realized that the youngster was ready for a regular school, but the base school was only for the dependents of American personnel. A sympathetic principal listened to Werr's pleas to allow Joseph in, then agreed to test the boy's knowledge in some basic subjects. A few weeks later, Joseph was sitting in a fifth-grade classroom.

One day, when Joseph was talking about America, Werr took the opportunity to ask some questions of his own. Since his arrival, Joseph had made no effort to look for the relatives he had said lived in the Fukuoka area. This had always troubled the chaplain and now he wanted to find out what really was going on.

"What about your relatives in Japan?" he said. "Wouldn't you like to find them?"

When Joseph didn't answer, Werr asked him why he hadn't looked for his family.

At that moment, Joseph knew he could no longer continue lying, especially not to a person who had become like a brother. With tears welling in his eyes, Joseph blurted out everything, how he and the Korean interpreter had made up his story so he could get to Japan.

Joseph said he didn't want to lie. But if he hadn't, he would still be in Korea. And he wouldn't have found Father Werr, his "brother."

Under regulations, the chaplain should have turned the boy over to the Japanese authorities for deportation to Korea. Under regulations, any obligation Werr had toward the boy should have ended. Under regulations, Joseph's dream of going to America should have been snuffed out. But Werr was not angry. Actually, he was relieved. He felt that a weight had been lifted from their relationship, and that Joseph had put his total trust in him.

Joseph asked Werr if he would help him get to America.

Werr told Joseph about all of the obstacles — the distance, the expense of flying, the immigration laws, and the difficulty in gaining permission to enter the country. It might take years to make the arrangements and even then, there was no guarantee that things would work out.

Werr said he would try his best. In the meantime, Joseph had to continue to study and to learn as much English as possible. If the miracle happened, he had to be ready.

Over the next few months, Werr wrote letters. He wrote to President Truman, whose office put him in touch with the State Department. The State Department then put him in touch with the U.S. consulate in Korea. The consulate told him that the quota for Korean nationals wishing to enter the United States was filled for the next nine or ten years. There was nothing that could be done.

Werr figured it would take an act of Congress to get Joe into the United States. That would mean lots of paperwork and red tape. So he began asking people who knew the boy to write letters about the boy's character, intelligence, and desire to make a home in America. He gathered reports, health certificates, recommendations, and other records that would be needed should there be an opportunity to plead the boy's case to someone who could help. Soon, Werr had a bulging file of papers and letters about Joseph.

In early 1953, Werr was temporarily assigned to another base in northern Japan. Major William Powers, another chaplain, took Werr's place at Itazuke. Werr asked Powers to keep an eye on Joe, then mentioned that he was trying to get the boy into the United States. Unfortunately, Werr didn't know a congressman who could pull the necessary strings.

Powers said he didn't know any congressmen either. But his brother did. Powers offered to ask his brother to write to the senator, Homer Ferguson.

A few weeks later, a letter from Sen. Ferguson was delivered to Werr. The senator said he was interested in the boy's case and listed all of the documents the senator needed. In addition to the paperwork, the senator had to have an assurance that if Joseph was admitted to the United States, he would never become a public charge.

To Werr, adoption seemed to be the most logical choice. But then an Air Police officer suggested Boys Town, where Joseph would be with kids his own age.

Werr quickly contacted Monsignor Wegner at Boys Town and laid out the situation. In two weeks, Werr had an answer: Boys Town would take Joseph.

With the assurance that Joseph would have a home in the States, Ferguson began working on special legislation to allow Joseph into the United States. But then, by accident, he found out that one spot had opened up on the Korean quota for that year. Ferguson urged Werr to quickly contact the U.S. consulate in Fukuoka. Werr telephoned the consulate and the next day heard the news he thought he would never hear: Joseph Anthony was on the list for immediate travel to the United States as a permanent resident. It was May 1953.

Werr had not told Joseph about the work and planning that had been done in the months since the priest had agreed to help the boy. The chaplain didn't want to get Joseph's hopes up in case things didn't work out. And Joseph hadn't asked any questions or pressed his friend for information.

So Joseph didn't pay any attention when someone delivered a note to his teacher one day in late May. It wasn't until the teacher stepped to the middle of the room and asked for the students' attention that he looked up from his work. Then, she announced that Joseph Anthony would soon be leaving for the

United States. The students erupted in cheers and applause as Joseph sat motionless at his desk.

In the next few days, everyone on the base pitched in to help Joseph get ready for his trip. Someone got a half-fare ticket from an airline. The communications unit gave the boy a new radio and some men in an antiaircraft unit built him a wooden foot locker. The base held a casino night and raised $500 to help pay for the airline ticket; Joseph got the $200 that was left over for clothing and other necessities.

A week later, Joseph and Werr traveled to Tokyo, where Joseph would leave for the United States. The two friends spent a last day together, sightseeing and talking.

It wasn't until Joseph was to board the airliner that he began to cry. He wrapped his arms around Werr, hugging him tightly. Then he got on the plane. Werr saw the boy's face in a window before the Stratocruiser rolled to the runway and lifted off into the dark sky.

On June 11, the last long leg of Joseph's journey was completed when his plane landed in San Francisco. Joseph had reached his promised land.

Father Powers, whose brother had contacted Sen. Ferguson, met Joseph at the airport. The two flew to Scott Air Force Base in Bellevue, Illinois, where Powers was the chaplain. Joseph stayed there several weeks before heading to Boys Town.

Monsignor Wegner was on hand to greet Joseph when he arrived on June 30, 1953. In the morning, there was an orientation and testing to determine Joseph's school grade level. An intelligence test showed he had an IQ of 124. By that afternoon, Joseph was swimming at the Boys Town pool and being dunked by the other boys — their way of welcoming the new kid.

In the year he spent as a seventh-grader at Boys Town, Joseph was an exceptional student. He enjoyed collecting holy cards, taking photographs, and playing sports. He became an altar boy and served Mass regularly. Wegner referred to him as one of the best and brightest boys at Boys Town.

Joseph's arrival also sparked a lot of publicity about him and about Boys Town. In the fall of 1953, the Air Force sent a film crew to Nebraska to make a movie about Joseph and his journey to America. A *Saturday Evening Post* article about Joseph's life generated hundreds of letters from people who wanted to be the youth's pen pal. Many people donated money to a fund that had been set up for Joseph. Everyone who wrote said they had been inspired by his courage and determination.

In June 1954, at age 14, Joseph left Boys Town and went to Illinois to live with a foster family. The arrangements were made by Father Werr, who had returned to his teaching post at Quincy College in Quincy, Illinois. Werr had promised to provide Joseph with a college education if he ever got to America, and he wanted Joseph to eventually attend Quincy.

Joseph graduated from Notre Dame High School in Quincy four years later. He attended college there, majoring in political science and writing a book about his life. He also appeared on numerous television programs, including *This Is Your Life*.

In 1958, Joseph Anthony took his oath of citizenship. Donald Werr, who by then was Joseph's legal guardian, was there to see a dream fulfilled.

After graduating from college, Anthony taught American government and history at Guilford High School in Illinois for several years. He married his high school sweetheart, started a family, and later opened a small jewelry shop in Rockford, Illinois.

As an adult, Anthony became determined to return to Korea, possibly to find out what happened to his family. Incredibly, after a 10-year search that began in 1966 and included 11 trips to South Korea, he located his parents and a brother near the village of Taegu. Two years and a mountain of red tape later, he was finally able to bring his parents, his brother, and his brother's wife and four children to the United States.

During his early years in the United States, Anthony was

asked hundreds of times how he felt about living in the United States. This is how he once answered that question:

"I now hear church bells instead of fearful machine-gun shots. I read newspapers instead of propaganda leaflets. I speak freely instead of hesitantly. I walk with pride instead of suspicion. I live in a home instead of a hut. I eat three full meals instead of two soup meals a day. I experience laughter instead of tears. I know kindness instead of bitterness. All these and so much more make up the voice of democracy that is constantly making a deep impression on me."

Spoken like a true American.

Above and beyond the call

Boys Town citizens who fought in the Korean War served bravely and honorably. But some distinguished themselves in the line of duty, displaying extraordinary courage and dedication. Two such former boys were Lavern Bush and Arnold Lederer Jr. Their actions exemplified the spirit of sacrifice and dedication to duty they learned at Boys Town. These are their stories.

Lavern Bush came to Boys Town in 1943, a stocky 15-year-old who had lived in a children's home in Sioux Falls, South Dakota, all his life.

Lavern and his brother were only infants when their father left the family, leaving their mother unable to care for them. Life in the children's home was all right, but Lavern decided before he started junior high school that he wanted to go to Boys Town. He had heard about how other boys had found a home there and how great its sports programs were, and he wanted to be a part of that. In fact, when he wrote a letter asking Boys Town to admit him, he offered to pay $15 a month out of the money he had saved while working for a freight carrier.

Lavern did a lot of things well at Boys Town. But he excelled at football. A six-foot, 178-pound tackle, he was named to the Nebraska All-State team in 1945 and 1946, and was a key player on Boys Town teams that went 21-1 and won a share of the state championship those two years.

"He was aggressive from a defensive standpoint with a fast charge," wrote Gregg McBride, an Omaha sportswriter who chose the all-state teams. "He was consistent in all games, an excellent blocker on the line and downfield, and signal caller."

Those were the days when Boys Town was a national powerhouse in football. Father Flanagan did much to promote the values and reputation of Boys Town through its sports teams, especially the football program. In addition to playing Nebraska high schools, Boys Town teams traveled to major cities across the country to compete against other teams.

Lavern and his teammates were honored guests wherever they went. They enjoyed the privileges of sitting in on a session of Congress, eating lunch with generals and politicians, and visiting famous historical sites. On one trip to California, the team visited a movie set and met Spencer Tracy, who had portrayed Father Flanagan in the 1938 movie, *Boys Town*.

And people came to see them play. In 1945, Boys Town played in front of 100,000 people during a 12-game season, including a game against Detroit Central Catholic High School that drew 35,000 people.

Lavern was an avid stamp collector and was known as somewhat of a wit at Boys Town. The *Boys Town Times* newspaper once said of him: "With Bush around, anything can happen and it generally does." A counselor wrote that Boys Town would remember Lavern as "a rugged individual who was hard to influence but friendly and hard to dislike. He lived his life and there wasn't much to-do about it."

Lavern had his share of problems at Boys Town. He sometimes lagged behind in his school work and he didn't always follow the Home's rules. In 1945, Father Flanagan discharged Lavern from the Home for his role in a scheme to sell stolen Boys Town Honorary Citizenship cards.

For a while, it looked like Lavern's dream of graduating from Boys Town was over. But a short time later, after Lavern left Boys Town to work in Kansas as a harvest hand, an Omaha woman found out about his discharge and wrote a letter to Father Flanagan. She asked the priest to reconsider and give the boy another chance.

Lavern also asked Father Flanagan to forgive him and let him return to Boys Town. The priest agreed to let Lavern come back, but he placed him on probation and told him that he had to be a model Boys Town citizen.

Boys Town is a place of second chances and Lavern made good on his. He served as a village and police commissioner, excelled in football, and graduated with his class in 1947.

Unfortunately, his sports career ended the next year when he was injured during spring practice while trying to make the University of Nebraska football team. With no scholarship, Bush was forced to attend classes during the day and work at the railroad yard at night to earn tuition money. Eventually, the strain got to be too much and he had to quit school.

In June 1948, Bush enlisted in the Army. He was assigned to the 23rd Infantry Regiment as a machine-gunner.

Bush knew the legacy of Boys Town citizens who had been in the military. Nearly 800 had served during World War II, and 40 had been killed. He had been around when the boys returned home to Boys Town from the war. There had been many joyous homecomings. Father Flanagan had welcomed them, listened to their stories, and introduced them to the lads who were living there at the time. In the eyes of those young boys, they all were heroes.

When Bush joined the Army in 1948, the world was more or less at peace. The United States had emerged as the most powerful nation in the world after World War II. A new organization, the United Nations, had been created to help countries settle their differences peacefully.

Bush quickly adapted to the routine of Army life. But it wasn't long before a new flashpoint erupted in Asia. In July 1950, shortly after Communist North Korea invaded South Korea, Bush's regiment was ordered overseas to join America's allies in trying to repulse the North Korean army.

For the men in Bush's company, the first days on the front lines were confusing and frightening. Few of them had been in combat, and seeing dead American soldiers for the first time was a shock to many. Survival, both physical and mental, depended on toughness, and it wasn't long before Bush was a hardened combat veteran. When asked how he felt to be part of the United Nations "police action," the former Boys Town police commissioner referred to Korea as "a long beat, tough neighborhood."

On September 13, near the Naktong River, Bush was seriously wounded in a firefight. He was transported to a military hospital in Tokyo, where he spent more than a month recovering before returning to duty at the front.

A few months later, Bush wrote to Monsignor Wegner at Boys Town.

> Having a fine time here in Korea. Lots of excitement, just what I like. Hope you're having the same.
>
> I got out of the hospital in Japan and got back with my outfit just in time for the big battle way up north in which we got clobbered all over the place. We left enough equipment there to supply an army, including our personal belongings and also a letter from some man in Baltimore, Md. who got my name from you. Line us up again because I don't know his address.

> This thing over here is turning out to be
> a statesman's war with dire results for the
> old boys in the line who catch all the hell.
> We're moving again in a short while but don't
> know where. The last couple of days I've been
> scrounging around for chickens and collected
> 18 of 'em. Our squad already had one big
> chicken dinner, and we're planning another.
>
> I'm a BAR (Browning automatic rifle)
> man and I'm really a hot rod with it. By the
> way, I know you'd like to meet our regimental
> chaplain. He's been over here for 15 years;
> his name is Father Frank. He captured some
> 70 enemy soldiers when we were down on
> the Naktong River. I'm afraid he's getting too
> old for this rugged life, but he sure is keeping
> pace. I'll have to close for now so say hello to
> everyone for me.

As the months passed, Bush's unit saw more action as American and South Korean forces started driving the Communists northward. In February 1951, they were facing thousands of Chinese troops near Chipyongni, a strategic South Korean town. Eventually, a fierce battle for the town erupted as the Chinese encircled the Americans and a French batallion and tried to push them out with a series of night attacks.

The Chipyongni perimeter was dominated by rugged, hilly terrain. Both sides knew the importance of holding the high ground, so there were constant seesaw battles as the Communists and the U.N. forces fought to take or retake the most strategic hills. Although outnumbered and surrounded, the American and French forces held onto their positions, supplied by air drops from American transport planes.

Bush's company was under the command of Lt. Col. James Edwards. Edwards called Bush "one of my favorite fighting men" because of the young soldier's spirit and enthusiasm. There was even a running joke between the two men. Bush had a habit of "losing" his helmet. When that happened, Edwards would pull a

spare that he kept in the back of his Jeep and toss it to the grinning GI.

One night, Bush and his machine-gun squad were preparing for another of the enemy's nightly attacks on their hill. A
Chinese soldier began firing near their position, but the
Americans held their fire. They knew it was a trick to get them
to fire back so the enemy could pinpoint their heavy weapons.

As Bush peered out into the darkness, he saw two Chinese
soldiers crawl to the double-apron barbed wire strung below his
squad's position. With two .50-caliber machine guns poised and
ready, Bush and his men watched as the pair set an explosive
charge under the wire. When the charge exploded, the Chinese
would rush through the gap and try to take the hill. Bush's squad
would have to stop them.

As the seconds ticked by, Bush tried to keep his men calm.
"Not yet, not yet," he whispered.

Suddenly, a sharp crack split the night air. The wire
breached, a Chinese assault company that had been waiting just
down the hill sprang up and rushed toward the opening.

"Let 'em have it!" Bush yelled. Both machine guns opened
up as the first Chinese soldier cleared the gap. The staccato
pounding of the guns mixed with the screams and groans of the
attackers who were caught in the open by a hail of bullets. Then
an American rifle company opened fire, adding to the fusillade.

The next morning, the bodies of 16 Chinese soldiers lay in
the gap in the barbed wire. Another 86 were sprawled in a nearby draw, cut down before they could even reach the opening.
Bush's squad had smashed the attack.

For his outstanding leadership in the face of the enemy
attack, Bush received the Distinguished Service Cross, the sec-
ond-highest citation awarded for valor in combat.

Bush would see much more fighting before his tour ended
in September 1951. Two days after writing the following letter,
he was seriously wounded in action near the Inje River.

Dear Father Wegner,

It's been a good while since I last wrote you, so I guess I'd better drop you a line and let you know how I am. I completed a full year of front line duty this Aug. 5 and I'm still going strong; enough said!

We just switched sectors of the line we occupied with the French. Right now we're somewhere north of northwest of the Inje River, on a high ridge of hills overlooking a big valley we call "The Punchbowl." We usually get to play tag with the enemy at night to keep things exciting. For the past month, though, there hasn't really been anything going on. Everybody seems to be waiting for the outcome of the peace meetings.

The last three days, I've gotten three different letters with applications for membership in the Boys Town Alumni Association. If you don't mind me giving my opinion, I think it is a very good idea and it's high time someone got around to doing it. After all, the ultimate value of all the training a boy gets at the school is determined in the years after he leaves.

I'll have to close now. It looks like rain and I haven't got my hole fixed yet.

P.S. I made Sgt. not long ago — it was a long time coming but it finally did.

Bush returned to the United States from Korea in September 1951. In addition to the Distinguished Service Cross, he had earned other medals and citations, including the Bronze Star, the Korean Service Medal, the Korean Presidential V Citation, the Croix de Guerre (awarded by the French), and two Purple Hearts for wounds suffered in combat. He was discharged from the Army in 1954 but later re-enlisted and served a tour of duty in Vietnam, where he was wounded in action.

In 1969, after his discharge from the service, Bush returned to Boys Town to work as a counselor. When Boys Town switched to its Family Home program in the early 1970s, he and his wife became Family-Teachers, living and working with troubled kids. Bush later took a position as a Boys Town police dispatcher. He retired in 1992 after giving 23 years of service to the place that had once been his home.

★   ★   ★

Arnold Lederer Jr. was 24 when an enemy bullet cut him down on a Korean battlefield.

In his short life, Lederer served in two wars and three branches of the service. As a member of the U.S. Coast Guard during World War II, he was temporarily blinded in action off Okinawa and received the Bronze Star for bravery. He served a three-year hitch in the U.S. Marines after the war, then joined the Army in 1949. In Korea, he won another Bronze Star, this time for maintaining a communication line between a command post and a rifle company during an enemy tank attack that wiped out his entire squad.

Lederer's final act as a soldier earned him the Silver Star for gallantry. On September 13, 1950, he volunteered to lay a telephone wire from a command post to a forward company that was attacking enemy positions. As he maneuvered toward the front line under heavy fire, he suddenly was hit. Though mortally wounded, Lederer continued on to deliver the telephone line to the forward position. He died a short time later.

Lederer's younger brother, Harold, was about 500 yards from the spot where Arnold died. Both young men were with the 27th Infantry Regiment and had watched out for each other whenever possible. But there was nothing Harold could do for his brother. Wounded himself, Harold had to be evacuated out of the battle area to a hospital in Japan. Later, he would receive the Bronze Star.

Arnold and Harold had always been close. Growing up in

Kansas City with their mother during the Depression, they had learned to depend on each other as friends as well as brothers. They came to Boys Town in 1939, sent there by their mother who was worried that she couldn't care for them properly.

During their three-year stay at Boys Town, they were well-behaved, modest, and well-liked. They returned home to their mother in 1942, but Arnold continued to write to Father Flanagan, even after joining the Coast Guard and being sent to the Pacific in 1943.

In 1946, Father Flanagan received the following Christmas letter from Arnold, who was then stationed in California.

> Just a line to let you know that I received your swell Christmas card. There is not very much news from around here. As you can see, I have a new address. Boy have they been moving me around.
>
> Tonight I am going to midnight Mass. Sure wish that I could be at Boys Town and go to the midnight Mass. There are two things that I really am going to pray for tonight and one is that there will be places all over the world like Boys Town. You have done a lot of good work for me and the many other boys who went through Boys Town and you are also going to do a lot for the many other boys who are going to pass through there. The other thing is that there will not be another war like the one we just had.
>
> Well, Father, I will close for now. Will write again soon.
>
> One of your boys,
> Arnie

Harold joined the Army in 1945. Eventually, he and Arnold got assigned to the 23rd Infantry Regiment. When the Korean War started, their regiment was one of the first to see action.

While Arnold always seemed to be in the middle of the action, Harold had his share of close calls. too. In summer 1950, after an attack on an enemy position, Harold was firing from a foxhole when an enemy bullet ripped through the top of his helmet. The bullet knocked the helmet 30 feet behind the 22-year-old corporal and singed his hair but otherwise left him unharmed.

Harold later told a war correspondent that the incident left him "shaking like a hula girl in a cold stream in the middle of winter."

For a long time after Arnold was killed, Harold would wonder why he had survived and his brother had not.

Several months after Arnold's death, his Silver Star was presented to his mother in a ceremony in Kansas City. Monsignor Wegner, Father Flanagan's successor, was on hand to pay tribute to a former boy who had dedicated his life to the service of his country.

"Arnold Lederer, by his outstanding bravery, will continue to live for generations in the memory of millions of grateful people.

"His dying legacy to these United States, its citizens, and especially the little citizens of Boys Town is an exalted example of a generous good life devoted to God and his country.

"Would that we all, from those who stand in the high places in the nation, to those in the most humble ones, might learn and take to heart what the death of each soldier, marine, and sailor means: and, that as they marched without fear to do battle, we may learn to act and walk in all honesty, integrity, doing our duties before God in the most conscientious manner, and so, with God's help solve the problems besetting the nation and help alleviate the sufferings and heavy heart of all people who wish to live in peace and harmony."

Harold Lederer survived the war and served in the Army for 24 years. He died in Tacoma, Washington, in 1991 at age 63.

Vietnam War

No event in recent times so deeply divided our nation as the war in South Vietnam.

Between August 1964, when large numbers of U.S. troops first were sent to the small Asian country, and January 1973, when the last troops were withdrawn, more than 58,000 Americans were killed and another 153,000 were wounded. Others who survived and returned home bore the war's emotional and psychological scars.

The conflict was marked by protest and political upheaval on the home front, and savagery and cruelty on the battlefield. There was uncertainty over America's involvement and how the war should be fought, and as the conflict dragged on and casualties mounted, more and more Americans questioned whether the sacrifice of American lives was necessary.

Vietnam was different from any war the United States had ever fought, especially at home. For the first time, television brought the sights and sounds of battle into America's living rooms every night.

Soldiers faced the steamy jungles, monsoon deluges, and rugged terrain of Southeast Asia, and an enemy that did not fight by the conventional rules of war. When they returned home, they often were met with silence, not the fanfare that greeted the veterans of earlier wars. Only in recent years have Vietnam vets been properly honored for their service and dedication.

Dozens of former Boys Town citizens fought in Vietnam; at least 17 were killed in action. Most of them were young men, each with a life of hope and promise ahead.

At home, the United States was going through a huge cultural upheaval in the 1960s and 1970s. There was a questioning of authority by young people, an increase in the use of drugs, and a growing mistrust of government.

Boys Town was going through its own changes. In the late 1960s, the Home started seeing more and more youth with problems that past methods could not resolve. A new way of caring for youth was needed. Within a matter of years, Boys Town had adapted a new treatment approach which became known as the Family Home program. The large dormitories and other institutional markings were replaced by homes where the youth could live in a family setting. Married couples, trained in teaching youth social skills, became the caregivers. The program, designed to help the youth change their behaviors, became the impetus for Boys Town to take the lead in changing how America cares for its children.

Leadership also changed at Boys Town. Monsignor Wegner retired as executive director in 1973. Father Robert Hupp, who would guide Boys Town for 12 years, was named as his successor.

When the last American troops pulled out of South Vietnam in 1975, Boys Town, like the rest of the world, was in a state of rapid change.

The soldiers wrote about the compassion and sympathy they felt for the South Vietnamese people they were trying to help. They told of the pain and suffering, and sometimes they quietly wondered why they were fighting.

Most letters were about going home.

A willingness to serve

When Captain Lowell Bittrich got to the top of Hill 65, most of the men of Charlie Company were already dead or wounded. A scant 21 remained on the hill, a few more were scattered nearby.

He added the 200 men of his own Bravo Company and dug in to help fight the estimated 1,200 Viet Cong (VC) and North Vietnamese regulars who surrounded Hill 65.

The men on Hill 65 had orders to leave, but they could not evacuate their dead comrades, and they would not leave without them. Standing by your friends, that was something Lowell Bittrich had learned many years ago at a place called Boys Town.

"At Boys Town there is a famous statue of one boy carrying another on his back," recalled Bittrich. "Written at the bottom of the statue are the words, 'He ain't heavy, Father, he's m' brother.' At Boys Town, we learned we had a responsibility to that guy standing next to us. It was a matter of honor to stand up for him. We were not willing to leave just because it was convenient."

Lowell first came to Boys Town from Fort Dodge, Iowa, when he was nine years old. His mother was divorced and trying to care for him and his sister Beverly. His local parish priest took him to Boys Town for a visit.

"I fell in love with the place," he remembered. "It was wide open to the sky and there were boys running all around. I lived in a poor section of Fort Dodge and I was always in trouble. All the kids were in trouble. This place looked like heaven to me."

Lowell was accepted into Boys Town. "I was already in some sort of trouble by the afternoon of my first day there," Bittrich laughed. "But I got better. By ninth grade I was a commissioner, the youngest and first on the grade school side."

The commissioners were highly respected members of the community. The boys elected the commissioners and the mayor to help Monsignor Wegner, the director of Boys Town in the 1950s and '60s, govern Boys Town.

Lowell ran the half-mile and quarter-mile races on Boys Town's high school track team. "I even tried to compete in the mile event one time," said Bittrich. "We had a guy named Charlie 'Deacon' Jones on the team back then who ran the mile for us. Deacon later went on to run in the Olympics. One race against him and I said 'no more.'"

Living at Boys Town was different from anything Lowell had ever experienced. "We had a lot of traditions there," he recalled. "It made it seem like family. During Christmas season, we had the twelve days of Christmas. I remember on St. Stephen's day, all the kids in the home named Steve gathered and we elected one king for the day. He could order us around for that one day.

"Then the next day he got put in the middle of a great big field with a fence all around him. Every one else stood outside the fence and threw eggs and tomatoes at 'King Stephen.' It was a real difficult throw, so we almost never hit the kid, but it was a lot of fun."

Lowell won a scholastic award for being one of the top ten boys in his class. When he graduated, Monsignor Wegner helped him get into Creighton University in Omaha, Nebraska. He came back to Boys Town in the summer and worked as a counselor for the boys. He was commissioned an officer by the ROTC program while he was at Creighton.

He arrived in Vietnam in May of 1965. For the first month his unit was restricted to the base. "We were supposed to protect the air base at Bien Hoa," said Bittrich. "They felt we needed to stay close."

Bittrich believes that the Americans were in a unique position when they first came to Vietnam. "There's an old Vietnamese saying," recalled Bittrich, "that says, 'The emperor's rule stops at the village gate.' These people had no relationship with the national government. The national government did nothing for them. We had an opportunity to make a real difference in their lives and we welcomed that chance.

"They called us 'sky soldiers' because the 173rd, my brigade, were paratroopers. They saw us coming down from planes and thought maybe we could do more for them than their own government. We tried to. Especially in 1965, they were why I was there."

In June of 1965, a South Vietnamese special forces camp near the town of Dong Xoai was overrun by the Viet Cong. Five South Vietnamese battalions went in to help regain the base and three were bloodily repulsed and destroyed.

"We sat on the Phuoc Vinh air strip for four days while those battalions were being destroyed," recalled Bittrich. "We watched it from the air but we had no authority to step in. I think that convinced the North Vietnamese that we weren't a serious threat.

"After that disastrous fight, we were given the authority to take the offensive. One of the first places they sent us was an area called War Zone D."

Near the Saigon River, it was an area of triple canopy jungle. Bittrich remembers it was like a "huge green bowling alley that a pale light filtered into. The space between the trees seemed straight and uniform, like alleys. It was only where the light leaked through that vegetation grew and cluttered up the jungle floor."

It was a stronghold formerly used as a redoubt by the Vietminh and Vietnamese bandits. Here the VC trained, treated their sick, launched their propaganda attacks on Saigon, and supplied their forces. Bittrich's 173rd Airborne Brigade was ordered to patrol it and try to clean it out step-by-step. In early November, 1965, the 173rd invaded War Zone D south of the Dong Nai River. Their first three days were quiet. On the fourth day, acting on an intelligence report, they encountered a large enemy force.

"We literally stumbled on their propaganda headquarters," said Bittrich. "Charlie Company had been sent out on a search-and-destroy mission. They were just about ready to return empty-handed when they thought they'd give the area one last look."

The VC headquarters had been dug into the side of a hill and was built in three levels underground. It was expertly camouflaged. During the search, one platoon of Charlie Company called a halt right on top of the enemy bunker. Fearful of discovery, the VC attacked.

"They cut off that platoon, wounding or killing our soldiers, almost to the man," recalled Bittrich. "At the time, my three platoons were moving in different directions ahead of me. When Charlie Company came under attack, we all moved to the sound of the guns."

When Bittrich got to the top of Hill 65, Charlie Company's commander, Captain Henry Tucker, reported that his company

Three former Boys Town boys lost their lives at Pearl Harbor on Dec. 7, 1941: George Thompson, Donald Monroe, and William Debbs.

Pfc. Bob Paradise (upper left, holding flag) and other liberated Bataan prisoner of war camp survivors celebrated in Manila on their way home to the States.
(Photo by P.R.O. AFWESPAC)

Cmdr. Lloyd Bucher talked with his USS Pueblo crew at the Balboa Naval
Hospital in San Diego after their release from North Korea. *(U.S. Navy Photograph)*

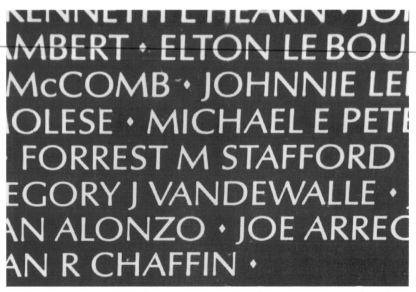

Medic Forrest M. Stafford, his name engraved on the Vietnam War Memorial in
Washington, was one of 17 Boys Town residents known to have died in service in
Vietnam.

Left: *Father Peter and Boys Town residents prayed for the safe return of alumni serving in the Persian Gulf War. A Christmas tree bedecked with yellow ribbons stood in Dowd Chapel until the war ended.*

Right: *Ray Huckeby served in an Army reserve transportation unit that convoyed water to the front lines in Saudi Arabia during Operation Desert Storm.*

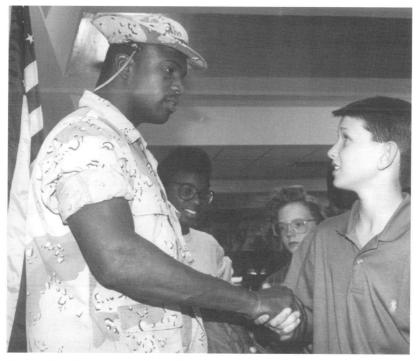

Marine Ron Dennis returned to tell Boys Town students of his part in the liberation of Kuwait.

Above: *Gen. Colin L. Powell, Chairman of the Joint Chiefs of Staff (with his wife Alma), spoke to Boys Town students during a June 1, 1992, visit.*

Below: *In July, 1991, Boys Town dedicated a memorial to the thousands of alumni who have served in the armed forces since its founding in 1917.*

Above: *Participating in the memorial dedication were representatives of the five military branches: Sean Dorcy, '88; Scott Swett, '90; Ron Dennis, '88; Richard Blackwell, '90, and Sam Rivers, '87, all on active duty at the time.*

was surrounded. Charlie Company was scattered by platoons, and casualties were high. They had walked into a hornet's nest of claymore mines and machine guns. The survivors sought what cover they could find, began firing back, and waited for help to arrive.

"When I got there all of Charlie Company's platoon leaders were wounded," said Bittrich. "Their executive officer had been hit in both hands. He was operating the radio while another man held the handset for him.

"The first thing I had to do was secure the perimeter and find his people. We called in the artillery and air power. They began to lay a wall of steel around us. If they hadn't supported us quickly, we might have been overrun then and there."

When the firing died down a little, Bittrich heard a strange sound. A bugle blowing in the jungle. He knew from old soldiers' stories of the Korean War, that that was the signal for a human wave attack by the enemy. The Americans tried to direct the highest firepower at the direction of the bugle calls and waited for the first attack.

Bittrich listened to the sounds of the enemy gunfire. He was trying to discover the size of the enemy force they were facing. "I knew there were no .50-caliber machine guns below the regimental level in their front-line units," said Bittrich. "I heard the firing of three distinct .50-caliber weapons coming from different directions and knew we were up against elements of three enemy regiments."

With the help of artillery and air power, the first attack was repulsed. The enemy quickly regrouped, leaving their trenches and blowing bugles, and launched themselves once again at the encircled Americans. "The noise was constant and awful," recalled Bittrich. The sounds of the weapons firing, bombs falling and the screams of the wounded combined to make a horrific sound.

Bittrich knew he had to keep his men on top of the hill. It

was the only tactical advantage he had. His men were severely outmanned and, at least on the ground, outgunned.

"I moved the men all over the place," said Bittrich, "but I kept them on top of that hill. The enemy could easily overwhelm us if they pinned us down so we had to keep moving. We also had to keep in motion so they couldn't get a fix on how few we actually were."

Successive waves of enemy soldiers burst and broke on Hill 65. Bittrich and his men often fought hand to hand. "There was a time when I was convinced we were all dead," said Bittrich. "None of us were coming out alive. The enemy just kept coming, and we were barely holding on."

All through that day the enemy assaulted the hill. They were turned back again and again by Bittrich and his men along with tremendous artillery and air support. When night finally began to fall, the fighting died down. Bittrich used the lull to try and evacuate some of the most critically wounded.

Medic Lawrence Joel, of Charlie Company, had personally saved over 30 paratroopers by dashing into enemy fire to rescue downed men. Wounded twice in the leg, he pulled the men to safety. He later received the Congressional Medal of Honor for his actions.

"There were five men that I knew were so critically wounded they wouldn't last the night without a doctor," recalled Bittrich. "There was no clearing to land a chopper so we improvised.

"They sent in some Air Force choppers that they used to put out aircraft fires. They lowered rescue baskets down through the triple-canopy jungle until we could load the soldiers in them, and then they took off dragging the baskets through the treetops. All five men survived."

Charlie and Bravo Companies had been reinforced by Alpha Company. There were no longer any reserves in case of a final overwhelming assault. Fortunately, the enemy began to withdraw the next day. They had been savaged by American firepower and American willpower.

"The second day we opened a pad for one helicopter," said Bittrich. "We used chainsaws and dynamite to clear the zone. It must have looked like a pinpoint to those chopper pilots."

When the first chopper landed, one of its passengers was General Ellis Williamson, come to help evacuate the survivors personally. By risking his own life, the general made sure that the men on Hill 65 would be evacuated as soon as possible.

"Once we had a chance to sit back a little, we discovered why the North Vietnamese were so eager to recapture that hill," remembered Bittrich. "There was a treasure trove of information on their operatives there, including a list of all their Viet Cong agents in Saigon. The police used that list to capture and jail dozens of enemy agents."

For his actions, Captain Lowell Bittrich was awarded the Silver Star and his entire unit was given a Presidential Unit Citation. Writing to Monsignor Wegner in April of 1966, Bittrich expressed his gratitude for all of the support he'd received from Boys Town.

> . . . I would assure you and all the boys
> at home, that I treasure your letters more
> than any military award I have received.
> Many of the boys of the home have writ-
> ten me letters since I came to Vietnam and I
> have tried to answer them all. Just receiving
> these letters has encouraged me through
> many a difficult time and I believe they have
> done much to make my efforts worthwhile.

Bittrich returned to the United States in the spring of 1966 but he was back in Vietnam in October of 1967 for his second tour. Things had changed in Vietnam but the biggest change was just a few months away.

Just after Christmas of that year, Bittrich wrote a letter to Monsignor Wegner at Boys Town.

> Once again from Vietnam I wish you and all your loved ones a blessed Christmas and a successful New Year. We appreciate your prayers and those of our boys at Boys Town.
>
> The situation has vastly improved since my last trip, and with continued support, hopefully the war can be ended within the next few years. The Viet Cong have suffered continuous defeats upon the battlefield and have no hope of a military victory. Their only hope seems to be in the political arena where we pray our leaders will have the courage to make those decisions necessary for a just and a lasting peace.
>
> Your efforts and those of the faculty at Boys Town are demonstrated by the conduct of more of our Boys Town citizens who are now in Vietnam. It is indeed a pleasure to say that they have been a credit to their home. They accept their responsibilities and are thankful for the opportunity to serve.

Boys Town had already lost several graduates in Vietnam. Giuseppe Gianelli was the first to be killed. Today there is a street named after him in the village of Boys Town. Forrest Stafford, a medic, was killed while trying to rescue wounded buddies. By the end of the war, 17 Boys Town graduates had given their life in service to their country.

Lowell Bittrich had known many of these men, and others as well. Men like Richard Girouard, who won a Bronze Star, and James Sampers, who was killed when the Jeep he was riding in was ambushed by the Viet Cong just outside of Saigon. Both men had left Boys Town the same year Bittrich did.

The war seemed to be going well for the Americans but in January of 1968 the Tet Offensive changed everything. Like

Bittrich, most in the military thought the end was in sight. They were ready to go home. The American public was becoming weary of the war and opposition to the war was building on campuses across the United States.

"Most of the time the enemy did not want to fight us," recalled Bittrich. "We had too much firepower for them. I think Tet was a desperate gamble to save the war for the North Vietnamese. They felt the only way they could win was to outlast us and they needed to show the people back home in America that, contrary to popular opinion, they weren't done yet."

Bittrich was at Chu Lai the night the Tet Offensive began. The tactical operations center at the base, which coordinated the division's operations, was hit with three rockets. No one was hurt, but communication was disrupted.

"The NVA and Viet Cong just wanted to pin the Americans down," said Bittrich. "They wanted to take on the ARVN (South Vietnamese) units. They felt if they could destroy the ARVN units the Americans would leave the war.

"It was a colossal failure of intelligence on our part. The signs of an imminent attack were all there. A few weeks earlier General Westmoreland had said he could see 'the light at the end of the tunnel.' When the American public watched Tet unfold on TV, there was disillusionment and disgust.

"It was a desperate gamble by the North Vietnamese. Their forces were decimated in the fight. Over 70 percent of the Viet Cong forces were destroyed. But they won the political battle. The American public wanted their wars to be convenient, one hour long with four commercial breaks and a happy ending.

"Tet was two weeks of intensive fighting. When it was over, the North Vietnamese had accomplished none of their military objectives. But politically, they had broken the back of American spirit. There was no good answer to why we were paying this price."

The war dragged on for five more years and Bittrich volunteered for a third tour in duty in 1971, but for him it was never the same. It was no longer fought by units which had been together for three years or more like it had been in 1965. "Now the soldiers served together for one year only and the average age was 19," said Bittrich. "The officers spent as little as six months with a unit. There was no cohesion, no *esprit de corps*."

For Bittrich it was always the men who were most important. "That's why I kept going back," he recalled. "I felt I owed it to these men. I didn't look at Vietnam as strictly a career move where you served for six months then hurried back to your desk job. I knew my troops would die for me, and I would die for them. I had to do whatever I could for them.

"In 1965 it had been so clear. We knew what we were fighting for, our country and each other. When we came down off of Hill 65 and back to our base, we knew what we had fought for.

"General Westmoreland came to our base and spent a whole day thanking each one of my men personally. I went down the line with him and introduced each man. I knew all their names. They were nervous about meeting the general but I told them to be proud and look him straight in the eye. The general was a soldier too, and he understood what they had just come through."

Bittrich's citation for heroism in the fight at Hill 65 reads, in part:

"Captain Lowell D. Bittrich has been awarded the Silver Star for gallantry in action in Vietnam.

"Captain Bittrich was assigned the mission to deploy his company into dense jungle terrain to search out and destroy a well-entrenched Viet Cong force. Upon making contact with the Viet Cong battalion, Bittrich's company came under intense hostile machine gun and automatic weapons fire. Quickly, he made an estimate of the situation, deployed his platoons to effectively counter the insurgents, and secured key positions.

"When the Viet Cong attacked from strongly fortified and well-concealed positions, Captain Bittrich's fearless and forceful leadership inspired his men to defend their ground under murderous fire. During the course of action he personally supervised his forward elements against five suicidal assaults which the Viet Cong organized and deployed in human waves.

"Each of the assaults was repelled with tremendous losses inflicted upon the insurgents. On the following day, Captain Bittrich organized and personally led several platoons into the insecure forward area to recover friendly casualties.

"His courage and determination led to the eventual defeat of the Viet Cong in that area. Bittrich's heroic actions were in keeping with the highest traditions of military service and reflected credit upon himself, his unit and the United States Army."

It was a willingness to serve and a devotion to his men that kept Lowell Bittrich returning to Vietnam.

"If you were wounded in battle you could go home," recalled Bittrich. "It all changed later, but in 1965 the men in my unit were reluctant to go home. They felt like they were abandoning their buddies.

"There was a young sergeant in my unit who was hit three times. The third time was a bad stomach wound. I went to see him at the hospital, and he pleaded with me, 'Sir, you can't make me leave my unit.' I told him, in no uncertain terms, he was going home. I didn't want to be the one who had to write his wife and tell her 'the fourth one did it.'

"A couple of years later, I was walking with my wife back in Ft. Campbell, Kentucky, and this young lady ran up to me and gave me a big hug and a kiss.

"I didn't know her so it shocked me a little. It was the sergeant's wife. She told me I'd saved her husband's life.

"I don't know . . . maybe I did."

Promises
to keep

Ken Suddeth can't remember the face of his mother or father. He doesn't know where he was born, or if he has any brothers or sisters. His earliest clear memory is of running down a mountain road in Korea.

"There were thousands of people and we were all running. People carried their belongings on their back or pushed them in small carts. Behind us we could hear the 'krump, krump' of enemy artillery and the sound of small arms fire. I remember seeing dead bodies in the ditches on the side of the road. Sometimes a plane would fly low and shoot at us. We would scatter when we saw one coming.

"There were thousands of people with me but I was alone. I had no family, no one who knew me. I was three or four years old."

Along with many other refugees, Ken eventually ended up at the South Korean seaport of Pusan. Pusan was one of the few secure areas in South Korea. The Allied soldiers went through here on the way to the front so it bustled with equipment and soldiers.

The train station was the real hub of activity. That's where he and hundreds of other street children congregated. They were looking to make some money or get a scrap of food from a generous soldier.

"I had been born in the country," said Suddeth. "The city was strange to me, but I found a way to survive. Really, we all just existed."

For two years Ken wandered the streets of Pusan and slept in the train yard with the other orphans, finding whatever cover and warmth he could from the harsh Korean nights. "It was so cold sometimes," he recalled, "you didn't really sleep. You just laid there awake, shivering until the morning came."

It was one of those mornings when Ken awoke at 5 a.m., too cold to lay still any longer. He needed to get up and move around. He saw an American soldier walking past and he spoke the only two words of English he knew, "GI. Chocolate?"

"The soldier stopped and looked at me," said Suddeth. "I don't know what he saw in me. I'm sure I was dirty and ragged and thin. He motioned for me to follow him and I did."

The soldier found a buddy who knew some Korean and he told the little boy that he needed a bath and then he was going to get him some clean clothes and some hot food. "I felt so lucky," remembered Suddeth. "There were hundreds of others just like me at that train station, but this soldier had picked me."

The soldier's name was Sergeant John Suddeth and he was with the 24th Infantry. Eventually he would give Ken Suddeth his name, for now he gave him a home. He lived on the base with the soldiers of the 24th Infantry and they called him "Champ." They introduced him to hamburgers and french fries and taught him about American music and American football. It was 1951, he was warm and safe, and he wasn't hungry anymore.

Halfway across the world Leo Magers was in his senior year at Western Kentucky University. He had come to Western Kentucky on a football scholarship. A scholarship he earned with the skills he had learned on the playing fields of Boys Town.

Leo Magers' father had been a career Marine. He had fought against the guerrillas in the nationalist insurrection in Nicaragua in the 1920s and had married a Nicaraguan woman. Magers himself came along late in his father's life and was born in Quantico, Virginia. When his father retired from the service, he moved his family to a small town in the hill country outside of San Antonio, Texas.

"It was hard for my parents," Magers recalled. "My father was no longer a young man, and my mother had a mental relapse after suffering a stillbirth. I didn't have any proper supervision, and I began to run the streets. By the time I was 11, I had spent time in jail for stripping cars and getting in fights.

"People tried to help me. My first probation officer was current Congressman Henry B. Gonzales. He did what he could. I still get Christmas cards from him. But I was just too wild."

In 1945, when he was 13, Leo and another boy ran away to New Orleans. They stole a suitcase from a man in the train station and were picked up by the police.

Alone and far from home, Leo stood in the probation officer's office. "I remembered seeing the old 1938 *Boys Town* movie and I mentioned it to the probation officer," said Magers. "He got in touch with the Catholic Welfare Bureau, and they got in touch with Boys Town. I was there before the year was out.

"The first couple of weeks at Boys Town were rough. I thought I was a tough guy, and I didn't think I should have to work like everyone else. That was bad enough, but then I made a wrong comment about one of the black kids there and I learned the hard way what real trouble was.

"I began to try and get along with everyone. I knew there was a price to pay if you didn't. These guys became my brothers."

There is a whole system of tunnels running under ground between Boys Town's buildings. They carry the water, heat, and power lines between the buildings. Now they are locked tight and secured, but in Magers' day they were still occasionally left unlocked.

"Me and a bunch of other guys got into those tunnels one day around Christmas time. We started to wander around exploring and opening doors. We opened the door to the post office, and we found some Christmas packages there. I took one that belonged to Father Flanagan.

"We didn't know it was a federal offense. I got in so much trouble for that little escapade. They had me collecting garbage around Boys Town every day for a month. I was real close to being sent away from Boys Town and I knew it. I decided I had to do something about it.

"I went to Father Flanagan's office, and there were two congressmen waiting to see him. But Father Flanagan's policy was always to see the boys first. He asked, 'Who's out there?' They told him me and a couple of politicians, and he said, 'I'll see Leo first.'"

Leo told Father Flanagan that he was scared he was going to have to leave and that he wanted a second chance. "He put his arm around me," Magers remembered, "and he told me, 'OK dear, we'll let you stay. Just get your act together.' From that day on, I walked the straight and narrow."

Leo was as good as his word. He was eventually elected a commissioner and graduated in the top ten in his class. Along the way he found time to play a little football, just like Ken Suddeth would almost 20 years later. Leo played halfback on the powerhouse Boys Town teams of the 1940s.

"No one in Omaha, except one school, would play us in football. We were so good. We went all around the country playing big prep schools.

"The movie had made Father Flanagan a celebrity so we got royal treatment almost everywhere we went. They usually had a big banquet for us, and everyone made speeches. I was just a kid but I thought it was great."

In the '40s, high schools in Nebraska had boxing teams just like they have wrestling teams now. In his senior year, Leo was state champion in the welterweight division.

Leo Magers had a very successful football career at Western Kentucky. He was named an honorable mention All-Conference his senior year. After graduating, he joined the Air Force and continued to play football. He made All-Air Force in 1956 and 1958 and was drafted by the Cleveland Browns and San Francisco 49ers. He was invited to spring practice with the 49ers but decided to accept a regular Air Force commission and was reassigned to an active flying unit.

Magers got in on the tail end of the Korean War. He served his tour of duty after flying school and returned home to his family in the United States.

Ken Suddeth was also headed for a new home in the United States. Ken had lived with the soldiers for three years and gotten to know Sergeant Suddeth very well. The sergeant told the young Korean boy that he wanted to adopt him and bring him home to America.

When his tour was up, Sergeant Suddeth left Ken behind in Korea while he went back home to arrange for an adoption. He returned to Korea within a year with adoption papers in hand, and the two set off for America.

"I was so scared," recalled Suddeth. "Everything was so different, and my English was poor. I depended on my father for everything. I had a lot of emotional and psychological adjustment to go through."

Ken moved to Columbus, Georgia, to live with his new father and mother, but things became difficult very quickly. His adopted mother was uncomfortable with this small Oriental boy in her home and his father was often gone. He began to stay away from home more and more frequently.

One thing his father had done was to take him to the Boys Club in Columbus. He made friends there and learned how to play football. When his mother and father divorced a few years later, his friends at the Boys Club helped get him to Boys Town.

It was hard for him to leave his father. He knew he was a good man, but things had just gotten too complicated. Ken Suddeth was 11 when he first came to Boys Town in 1960.

"I didn't want to go to Boys Town, I wanted to stay with my father," said Suddeth. "The first few weeks at Boys Town were very difficult. Every day I went to the hill overlooking the highway that led into Omaha. For hours at a time, I watched the cars go east and west, and I wished I was in one of them heading home. Except I wasn't sure where home was anymore.

"I remember feeling pretty sorry for myself until one day I walked past a playing field and saw some boys playing football and I thought, 'That looks like fun.' From that day on I decided to make the best of it where I was. And in the end Boys Town turned out to be the best thing that ever happened to me."

Ken got involved in sports. He wrestled, ran track, played football, and became a black belt in Tae Kwon Do karate.

He read history and American literature and fell in love with the poems of Robert Frost. "I loved his poem about 'promises to keep,'" Suddeth said. "I always felt I had a lot of promises to keep to God and the people who had helped me along the way."

Among those people who helped were an Omaha family who had befriended Suddeth after his freshman year at Boys Town. Bob and Jean Reilly and their 10 children opened their home to Suddeth, and he soon felt very comfortable in this bustling household. "The Reillys encouraged me to use my talents and skills wisely," said Suddeth. He soon became an unofficial member of the Reilly family.

He also became interested in politics and eventually was elected mayor of Boys Town in July of 1965. He was re-elected mayor the next year in 1966, one of the very few Boys Town mayors to be elected to two terms. In the spring of 1966, he became a U.S. citizen. Now he was not only the youngest mayor of any town in America, he was also a brand-new American citizen.

In his commencement speech, Ken thanked the staff at Boys Town for all the help they had given him through the years:

"We will try hard because we cannot fail those who taught us to be men, and those who follow after us. They are all Boys Town."

Suddeth originally planned to join the Army with a good friend from Boys Town. However, he changed his mind when he saw some of the special programs the Air Force offered and joined that branch of the service instead.

While he was stationed at McGuire Air Force Base in New Jersey, Suddeth met another airman who was going through training for a special unit called pararescue. They were the Air Force equivalent of the Green Berets. Suddeth was intrigued and decided to try and join the special unit himself.

After passing the swimming and endurance tests, Suddeth was given the chance to join a pararescue unit. The job of the pararescue units was to pick up downed pilots where they were, land or sea, and bring them safely back.

"I was very young," he said, "and I craved excitement and adventure. I thought this was the way to get it." Suddeth went through jump school, scuba diving school, survival and jungle survival schools. For Suddeth, it was all very challenging and also very thrilling.

Shortly after Suddeth arrived in Vietnam, the Tet Offensive exploded on the Americans and their allies. During the last two days of January, 1968, the North Vietnamese and their Viet Cong allies launched simultaneous attacks by 85,000 troops on five major cities, dozens of military posts, and over 150 towns and villages.

In one of the more grotesque episodes of the war, a fight between Marines and the Viet Cong took place in an old cemetery just outside Ton Son Nhut Air Base where Suddeth was stationed. In his book, *After Tet*, Ronald Spector describes the Marines and the Viet Cong crawling around behind gravestones while exchanging fire at close range.

"I was in Tan Son Nhut when the Viet Cong hit us," recalled Suddeth. "There were rockets all around, we just had to stay low and stay put. At first all the shelling drove me crazy, but eventually it got to be routine and I hardly noticed it."

For some other American forces the Tet Offensive was anything but routine. To the embattled Marines at Khe Sanh it was a daily fight for survival. They were aided in their struggle by the men of the United States Air Force, men like Colonel Leo Magers.

"I arrived in June of 1968, and I was flying reconnaissance missions very near Khe Sanh," Magers said. "I remember one clear night when there must have been a thousand B-52s heading north to bomb enemy positions outside Khe Sanh.

"They had bombed a crater around Khe Sanh so the North Vietnamese couldn't get to the Marines on top of the hill. I looked to my right, and the whole place was lit up like the Fourth of July. I couldn't believe they could get that many B-52s in the air at the same time."

The 6,000 Marines and South Vietnamese rangers at Khe Sanh were besieged by an estimated 40,000 enemy soldiers. They fought ferociously from the first attacks in early February until the base was finally abandoned on July 5, 1968.

Magers was stationed at Korat Air Base in Thailand. He flew reconnaissance missions along the Ho Chi Minh trail and into North Vietnam itself. He had gone through six months of survival school, jungle survival school, and air-sea rescue school. All to help prepare him to survive if his plane was shot down. Before his tour was over, Magers would fly 186 missions.

"We flew a lot of night missions, and you could watch the missiles and the 'ack ack' coming toward you," recalled Magers. "Along with radar and language experts, we had weapons control officers on the plane with us. When a missile was launched, you could pick it up on the radar. They'd call for a left turn and in a few seconds you could see the flash of the explosion off your right wing. Once we got high enough, the missiles and anti-aircraft fire couldn't touch us."

However, the MiGs, the Russian-built fighter planes the North Vietnamese used, were a different story. "We flew at about 300 miles an hour and they could fly at 600-700 miles an hour so you couldn't run away from them," said Magers. "They could close on the area where you were very quickly so you always had to be aware of them. You couldn't avoid them by simply flying high. However, by the end of the war they weren't much of a factor. They were no match for our fighter planes."

The plane that Magers commanded was an AWACs radar plane, the predecessor of the planes made famous in the Gulf War. The radar equipment was concealed inside the plane and was operated by highly trained specialists.

"Our missions were fully planned weeks in advance," Magers remembered. "On one particular mission, they sent frog men into the Mekong River basin, where it bisected the Ho Chi Minh trail.

"They placed small electronic receptors, designed to look like leaves, on the trees along the trail. As we flew over the area we were able to track vehicle and troop movement along the trail and sometimes even actual conversations."

Some of the information would show up in terms of latitude and longitude. Magers and his men would then translate this information to command headquarters who would use it for various military purposes.

"One of the more frustrating things was that there seemed to be two sets of rules," Magers said.

"I can remember one mission where we flew across the DMZ (de-militarized zone) north to Hanoi. We saw ships from countries who were allies of the Americans, unloading supplies into Haiphong harbor. We reported it back, but there was really nothing anyone could do.

"We had the firepower. We could have disrupted their supply lines easily and ended the whole thing, but we weren't allowed to use the full extent of our power. It made me start wondering what I was doing there."

Ironically, even though Magers risked his life on a regular basis flying combat missions, his two closest calls came in non-combat situations.

"My closest call came when some equipment in my plane malfunctioned," Magers said. "The plane went into a steep climb, and I couldn't get the nose down so I could land it."

"We were hurtling through the air and I thought, 'This is it, you just bought the farm.' I had no power steering. I finally got some control after a rapid descent, and I climbed back up to 10,000 feet and got the nose of the aircraft down. When we landed, we were all shaking." Magers received the first of his two Distinguished Flying Cross medals for his efforts in saving the lives of his 15 crewmen.

Magers' other close call came when he was visiting some South Vietnamese troops on an air base. The moped he was riding on was hit by a two-ton truck, and Magers was thrown under the wheels. Four of the truck's wheels were lying on Magers' left thigh when it stopped.

"When they finally got the truck off," Magers recalled, "my left leg was swollen to twice the size of my right leg. I was lucky though. Nothing was broken, just badly bruised.

"A pilot's greatest fear," said Magers, "is to go down in flames with no way out and no one to help you." It was the men in the Air Force's pararescue units, men like Ken Suddeth, who went after the pilots whose planes had gone down, into the jungle or into the sea.

"If you were a pilot," recalled Magers, "you had a lot of respect for those people. They went behind enemy lines in helicopters to rescue pilots. They gave you a sense of confidence. A feeling that you were not forgotten, that someone was coming to help you."

Before they went on a mission, pilots were briefed as to what areas they were to get to if they were shot down. They were given specific pick-up location coordinates and told to wait there for rescue.

"Of course the reality was that most times you were hanging in a tree with your beeper on, and they came and got you," Magers said.

When the pilots were wounded and unable to make it to the pre-arranged rendezvous, the pararescue units sent down a "penetrator."

Penetrators were large solid metal balls attached to the helicopter by an inch-thick cable. The penetrator had four sturdy metal seats which could be pulled out, like the leaves of an artichoke, and then clicked into place.

When a pilot was located, the penetrator was dropped, crashing through the jungle foliage. The rescuers would often use the cable to descend to the jungle floor. Once it was on the ground, the penetrator's seats would be clicked into place. Then the pilot would strap himself on and be hauled up to the waiting helicopter.

Kenneth Suddeth had followed a penetrator to the ground hundreds of times to rescue downed airmen. It was what he was trained to do. He believed in the pararescue motto, "That others may live."

"Typically," recalled Suddeth, "we'd get a call that a pilot was down and the nearest pararescue unit would be sent out after him. Often we went behind enemy lines to rescue these guys.

"Once we were behind enemy lines the Air Force and the government disowned us. We were no longer their responsibility. Officially we didn't exist. We knew the risk, and we chose to take it because we felt it was the right thing to do. We crossed that border and the adrenaline kicked in. We were bringing that man back.

"The saddest thing was when we'd get to the pilot and he'd already be dead. You'd think, 'Was it worth the risk?' But of course it was. That man's family needed to bury him and say good-bye properly."

Suddeth was also involved in many water rescues. The pilots usually ejected before the plane went down, but often lost consciousness. Their flotation devices kept them from drowning.

"It could be a very difficult rescue depending on the weather. We had to jump out of the 'copter in our scuba gear, cut the pilot's parachute and attach a rope for the chopper to pull him up.

"If the sea was rough, you couldn't use a rope. It was too difficult to balance between the waves and the chopper. In those cases you just inflated a portable raft and waited with the pilot until the sea calmed, and a rescue could be performed."

There were so many rescues sometimes they would blur a little in Suddeth's mind. But the bullet wound in his thigh always reminds him of the wounded major.

It was a black night. A canopy of clouds had blocked out what little light existed. Below in a rice paddy was a wounded pilot. They were 10 miles inside North Vietnam.

As the helicopter hovered overhead, Suddeth slithered down the rope to the side of the wounded pilot. Part of the major's arm was missing and his back was broken, but he was alive.

"He couldn't move himself and he was in a lot of pain, so I gave him a shot of morphine," Suddeth said. "There was no room on the rope for both of us, so I strapped him up and they carefully hauled him into the chopper. They were going to send another chopper back for me."

The North Vietnamese had heard the sound of the chopper. They were moving silently through the rice paddies toward the sound of the rotating blades and the man on the ground.

Suddeth tried to stay invisible, to fade into the black night. But the North Vietnamese knew where he must be, and they just sat and waited for the chopper to come back. Suddeth knew they were there. He could feel them watching him.

When the helicopter arrived, a rope was quickly dropped, and Suddeth moved through the plants and lunged for it. He hadn't climbed far when the night erupted in noise and flashes of light. They were shooting at him!

"I remember thinking I would never see daylight again," Suddeth said. "There was no way they could miss me. I got a round in my leg and it burned like crazy, but I kept climbing. As soon as I was pulled into the chopper, I passed out."

Before he left Vietnam in 1970, Suddeth was wounded twice. He received the Purple Heart, the Medal of Military Merit, and the Bronze Star. But to Suddeth, Vietnam was more than just war and enemies. There were also the native people of South Vietnam whom the Americans were supposed to be helping.

"I used to attend Mass whenever I could, " said Suddeth. "One day the Catholic chaplain announced he was going to the local orphanage to help the nuns fix the place up. He was looking for volunteers, and I signed up immediately."

It became a habit for Suddeth. At least once a week he would go to the orphanage to help out.

"When I found this place, it was very powerful for me. These kids were like me 20 years before. The same dirty faces, the same haunted look in their eyes. It was very emotional. I wanted so much to give back some of what I had gotten from others in my life."

He wrote Jean Reilly in Omaha and asked her to help. She began to collect old clothes in her neighborhood and sent them to Suddeth. "The war was hard to understand some times but this wasn't," said Suddeth. "I knew this. I knew these kids. This was me and my friends 20 years ago, and now I had a chance to help them.

"I watched the Vietnamese nuns give the clothes to these kids, and I felt incredible joy. This was humanity. I loved to watch them play while I painted and fixed up around the place."

Suddeth was keeping a promise. One he had made to himself years ago. Leo Magers keeps that promise too.

Magers lives in North Carolina now and works as a counselor for high-risk kids and potential high school dropouts. He helps them stay in school or get their GEDs. He is their counselor, their father figure, and their friend. Recently he was named Kiwanian of the year for his work with troubled youth.

Magers remembers a frightened boy in a New Orleans courthouse. He remembers a kindly priest who gave him a second chance. He sees himself in the children he helps. He has promises to keep.

Ken Suddeth also continued to work with troubled children. He was an officer with the juvenile court in Columbus, Georgia. He was elected Marshall of Muscogee County, Georgia, in 1992 – the first Asian-American marshall in Georgia history. He sees troubled kids every day, and he tries to help them. He has promises to keep.

Suddeth still remembers Robert Frost and his poem, especially the last few lines. "The woods are lovely, dark, and deep. But I have promises to keep. And miles to go before I sleep. And miles to go before I sleep."

★ t e n ★

Courage in captivity

Lloyd Bucher's spirits were sinking. He had promised himself he wouldn't let it happen, but he had started feeling sorry for himself and losing hope.

Staring out his cell door, Bucher tried to think of something positive, some sign that things were going to get better. As prisoners of the North Koreans, he and the 82 men in his crew had already suffered through months of beatings, interrogations, starvation, inadequate medical attention, threats of execution, and inhuman living conditions. When it became apparent that they could no longer endure the torture and mistreatment, Commander Bucher had allowed the men to sign confessions admitting that they were "criminals" and that their ship, the USS Pueblo, was spying in North Korean waters when it was captured on Jan. 23, 1968.

But Bucher and his crew were not criminals. While it was

true that the *Pueblo* was an intelligence-gathering ship on a mission to monitor North Korean and Soviet naval activity, the vessel was peacefully sailing in international waters when it was fired on and illegally hijacked by North Korean warships. What Bucher and his men signed were propaganda instruments that were full of obvious lies. When they were examined by U.S. officials, it would be clear that the *Pueblo* crew had been forced to comply with their captors' demands.

Bucher had been kept in a cell by himself most of the time since the crew had been moved to a prison camp near Pyongyang, the North Korean capital. Separated from his men, Bucher had no one to talk to, no one to offer encouragement. He knew he had to stay strong for himself and his crew. But there were times when pain, weakness, and despair seemed to be winning the battle. This was one of those times.

Now as he looked out his cell door, past the ever-present armed guard, one of his crewmen came into view. The man was on his hands and knees, crawling as soldiers prodded him along with their rifles. Blood dripped from his swollen lips.

"He had been beaten really bad," Bucher recalled. "His face was the size of a basketball."

Then the man turned his head.

"He looked at me and gave me a big grin and a thumbs-up sign. That really knocked my socks off. It taught me a lesson, and I promised to never let myself get down again."

Lloyd "Pete" Bucher had always been able to pick himself up when life knocked him down.

Born on September 1, 1927, in Pocatello, Idaho, Lloyd was abandoned by his 19-year-old unwed mother. Left in the hospital, he was soon adopted by a couple that ran a local restaurant.

When he was four, the boy's adopted mother died of cancer. Soon after, Lloyd's adopted father sent the boy to live with the father's parents on their Idaho farm. It was the first of many moves that would place the boy in three different households, a reform school, and an orphanage by the time he was eight.

The financial hardships of the Great Depression had a lot to do with Lloyd's being shuffled from place to place. While Lloyd was living with his grandparents, they lost their farm. They moved to Long Beach, California, where they managed an apartment court. It was there that Lloyd got his first look at an ocean, an event that triggered what was to be a lifelong love affair with the sea.

As the Depression worsened in the early 1930s, Lloyd's grandparents decided they just couldn't afford to continue to care for the boy. When he was five, they sent him to live with an aunt and uncle in Glendale, California. A year later, financial problems forced the aunt and uncle to put Lloyd on a train back to Idaho and his adopted father.

Things had gone downhill for the elder Bucher after his wife died. The restaurant the couple had operated went under, and he fell in with a group of men whose business dealings included sheep rustling and bootlegging. When Lloyd returned in 1934, his adopted father was living with the men in a cabin on the Snake River.

Seven-year-old Lloyd soon discovered that he would have to fend for himself. He fell in with a gang of youngsters who used a cave on the river as a gathering place. Since Lloyd was the only one of the bunch who could read, he would entertain the others with stories from pulp magazines they either stole or salvaged from the trash. Back at the cabin, Lloyd learned how to stay out of the way when the men had been drinking.

The situation took a turn for the worse when Lloyd's father was arrested for bootlegging and sent to jail. Since the other men had no use for the boy, they kicked him out.

So Lloyd made his home in the alleys of Pocatello, surviving on his wits and on handouts from restaurants.

One of his favorite tricks was to collect pop bottles and turn them in at a store for a few pennies. When the storekeeper put the bottles out back, Lloyd would grab them and head to another store for another refund. He also tried to live on the fish he caught in the river. But while stealing some new fish hooks at the five-and-dime one day, he was collared by a policeman and taken before a judge.

The judge sent him to a reform school, where as the youngest child he often was picked on by the older residents. Worried about his welfare, the authorities transferred Lloyd to an orphanage in Boise in 1935.

Now Lloyd faced a new peril — his religion.

"They had determined at the orphanage that I had been baptized Catholic," Lloyd would recall later. "There weren't many Catholics in Idaho in those days — mostly Mormons and Protestants. I was the only Catholic kid (in the orphanage) and when word got around, I was involved in fights about every day. I didn't even know what a Catholic was, but I knew it was causing me a lot of problems."

Luckily for Lloyd, a Catholic woman on the orphanage board realized what was happening and made arrangements for the boy to be sent to a mission home and school for children in Culdesac, Idaho. The home was on the Nez Perce Indian reservation in the northern part of the state, and was run by two Jesuit priests and nuns from the order of the Sisters of St. Joseph.

"It was really a fine place," Bucher recalled. "I was well taken care of and received the best schooling I could have gotten through the fifth, sixth, and seventh grades. I liked it there."

In school, Lloyd studied advanced subjects like algebra and Latin. The nuns helped nurture his love of reading, and his interests and academic skills soon were reaching beyond his grade level.

Lloyd was just getting used to his new home when a farmer and his wife in Washington State expressed interest in adopting him. But when they took him back to their farm, it soon became apparent that they wanted a farm hand, not a son. Lloyd ran away and made his way back to the mission home, 60 miles away.

Lloyd might have finished school at the home and gone on to a local high school had it not been for a movie that caught the nation's attention in 1938. The film was called *Boys Town*, and it told the story of Father Edward Flanagan, an Irish priest who had built a home for orphaned boys outside Omaha, Nebraska.

When Lloyd saw an article about the movie in a newspaper, he decided Boys Town was just the place for him. Besides, the high school there had a real football team with a real coach, and Lloyd loved football.

After talking to the mission nuns about Boys Town, Lloyd quickly sent a letter to Father Flanagan and the nuns contacted the priest about finding a place for the boy.

On a late summer day in 1941, 14-year-old Lloyd boarded a Union Pacific train bound for Omaha. (The mission nuns had convinced the railroad to donate a train ticket for Lloyd's journey.) The trip would take several days, and someone from Boys Town would pick him up at the depot.

But as the train chugged through the mountains of Montana, Lloyd started to have his doubts about this Boys Town. What if it was like the reform school or the orphanage he had been in? The more he thought about it, the more scared he got. So when the train made a stop in a small Montana town, Lloyd got off and started walking. He wasn't sure where he was going, but he wasn't going to Boys Town. Somewhere along the way he lost his train pass.

For two days, the boy wandered around alone. Finally, tired, cold, and hungry, he stumbled upon some hobos who were gathered near the train station. Lloyd told them he was supposed to go to a place for orphaned kids near Omaha, Nebraska. Two of the men decided to help the boy, and a short time later, the three travelers hopped on a freight train headed for Des Moines, Iowa.

In Des Moines, the two men convinced a trucker who was

driving to Omaha to take Lloyd with him. Finally, several days overdue at his destination, Lloyd arrived in Omaha. He walked the 10 miles to Boys Town, where he was met by none other than Father Flanagan.

"He told me that I was supposed to have been there several days earlier, and that he had been worried," Lloyd remembered. "I made up a story about how I had gotten off the train to use the bathroom and the train left without me, leaving me stranded."

With that bumpy start, Lloyd became part of the Boys Town family. At first, it wasn't quite what he had hoped for. Like everything else, the Home had been hit hard by the Depression and was just starting to come back from some tough financial times. It was still a time of doing without. For Lloyd, the biggest disappointment was the food. It wasn't very good, there usually wasn't enough of it, and the boys got meat only once a week.

"The big meal was the corn flakes we got on Sunday mornings after church," Lloyd said.

In those days, the boys ate their meals "family style" in the dining hall. At each table, the oldest boy served as a "table captain." He sat at one end and the youngest boy at the table sat at the other end. The captain got his food first, and if he liked it, there usually wasn't much left by the time it got to the other end.

Lloyd, who was one of those younger boys, was assigned the job of setting tables for Sunday morning breakfasts. Before long, he had figured out a way to get at least one filling meal a week.

"I would pour corn flakes in all the bowls. Then I would smash the flakes in my bowl with my fist, grinding them up so there was more room for more flakes. Once the bowl was almost full of the smashed flakes, I would pour some unbroken flakes on top to make my bowl look like everyone else's.

"I got so I could get almost a whole box of corn flakes in my bowl. We would be eating and everyone would be staring at me, wondering how I was able to keep eating for such a long time."

As time went by, the food improved and so did Lloyd's attitude about Boys Town. As more people became aware of Father Flanagan's work — due in large part to the publicity generated by the *Boys Town* movie — donations increased and the Home grew. Lloyd began to feel more like he belonged. He had a warm bed, he started making friends, and he liked school. And Boys Town was a place where a kid could get involved.

All his life, Lloyd had yearned to be accepted and liked. At Boys Town, he got his chance. He joined the Boy Scouts, served as class president or vice-president every year of high school, and headed almost every organization he was part of. He continued to be a voracious reader, and was almost unbeatable at chess. He started working on the Boys Town farm, earning five cents a day. And he started playing sports.

Lloyd had developed a love for football at the mission school in Idaho. The boys there had played touch football, though, and there hadn't been any organization or coaching. Lloyd had expected great things when he got to Boys Town, but the Home was so poor in the early 1940s that the football team had to practice in shifts because there wasn't enough equipment for everyone to suit up at the same time.

That all changed when Boys Town hired coaching legend Skip Palrang in 1943. Immediately, Palrang, who had coached at Creighton University in Omaha, dedicated himself to making Boys Town's sports teams the best. The Home bought new uniforms and equipment, and soon was developing what would become one of the finest football teams in the country.

Lloyd was a sophomore the year Palrang was hired. It was his first chance at making the varsity, and he was determined to be a starter. Small for a lineman at 160 pounds, Lloyd worked hard to learn how to use his speed, quickness, and intelligence to block bigger opponents. He enjoyed the teamwork and discipline that went with the sport, and Palrang became an important influence in his life as a mentor, coach, and friend.

When the 1943 season began, Lloyd was the starting left tackle, a position he would hold for the next three years. And his teammates had started calling him "Pete," after Pete Pihos, a college football player Lloyd admired. The nickname would stay with him his whole life.

Making the starting varsity team meant a lot to Lloyd. But there was an extra incentive for being a football player at Boys Town during that time. As a way to publicize Boys Town, Father Flanagan had for several years sent the football team around the country to play exhibition games against other high schools. For team members, that meant traveling to big cities, playing in front of huge crowds in famous stadiums, and seeing things they had only read about in books.

It was an opportunity Lloyd was not going to miss.

So with a new coach and a new attitude, Boys Town took its football program on the road. The team toured the East Coast by train for a month in the fall of 1943, playing in Boston, Washington, and Jersey City, New Jersey.

The next year, Lloyd and his teammates went to the West Coast, with games in Spokane, San Francisco, and Los Angeles. They also played in Detroit, where 45,000 people turned out.

"We outdrew every pro team in the country that Sunday," Lloyd recalled.

Everywhere the team went, the players were treated like kings. They stayed in fine hotels, had good meals, and got to meet celebrities. Once, after a game in Los Angeles, Spencer Tracy, who had portrayed Father Flanagan in the movie *Boys Town*, and singer Bing Crosby visited team members in their locker room.

For Lloyd, the experience was one of the most memorable of his life. He was a vital part of something important and worthwhile, and it gave him a great sense of accomplishment.

"It was the most glorious thing you could imagine for the kids who were on that team," he would say later. "We had some tough kids there. They knew how much they had to do to prove themselves. I think everyone of them benefited as a result."

Lloyd lettered three years in football and captained the team as a senior. He also lettered in track and played some basketball.

While Lloyd's athletic skills won him respect on the football field, he also was making a name for himself in the classroom. The courses he had studied at the Jesuit mission school in Idaho had been tougher than those at Boys Town, so he had little trouble getting good grades and consistently making the honor roll. He concentrated on science and technology classes to prepare himself for a career in engineering or geology, but also enjoyed learning about the arts, literature, and poetry.

He even enjoyed a year as a tenor with the Boys Town Choir. That involvement ended when the choir director, Father Francis Schmitt, had Lloyd sing a solo for him. "Pete," the priest said, using Lloyd's nickname, "you'd better stick to football."

In his senior year, Lloyd was elected mayor of Boys Town. In those days, being mayor was a high honor. Not only had you been elected by the other boys, but you also had a voice in decisions affecting the Home. Father Flanagan had always felt that self-government was an important way for the boys to learn responsibility and citizenship.

But Lloyd never had a chance to serve in the office. It seems that he and some other boys had made a number of unauthorized visits to Omaha and had befriended some girls who worked as ush-erettes at a local theater. The girls would sneak the boys into the movie, then sit with them in the back rows and "neck" when they weren't busy. Someone who knew Father Flanagan saw Lloyd with a girl and reported the incident to the priest.

"Nothing made him madder," Lloyd said. "That was a severe no-no. It cost me the mayorship. That upset me a lot but I just accepted it."

Lloyd had a few other close encounters with Father Flanagan during his stay at Boys Town. Several times he appeared before the student court for breaking rules (he ran away twice but returned on his own), and the priest personally handed down the prescribed punishment.

Another time, shortly after his arrival, Lloyd decided to go to confession at Dowd Chapel, Boys Town's Catholic church. As he walked in, he saw there were two lines — one with four or five boys and one that stretched from the confessional out the church door.

Lloyd got in the short line, wondering why the other line was so long. Not until he entered the confessional did he realize that Father Flanagan was on the other side of the screen.

"I told him I had a dirty thought. He came unglued in there. By the time he got through with me, I had a penance of about 30 days' worth of rosaries. He laid it on pretty thick."

Lloyd had learned why the lines were always longer with the other priests.

As he got older, though, Lloyd came to understand Father Flanagan and why he did what he did.

"Those were tough times," Lloyd would say later. "Everyone who was there needed to be there. He was providing a service that was unique. He was a strict disciplinarian but he was also a very caring person and, in his way, a loving person. He was a saint as far as I'm concerned. It was heaven on earth and I credit him for that."

During the four years Lloyd was at Boys Town, World War II raged in Europe and in the Pacific. Lloyd and all the other citizens of Boys Town were well aware of what was happening in places called Guadalcanal, Normandy, and North Africa. The young men of Boys Town were eager to do their part in the war effort, and in the summer of 1945, at age 17, Lloyd enlisted in the Navy. (He would complete his school work the next year and graduate as one of the top ten students in Boys Town's Class of 1946.)

Two years later, with the war over and the Navy reducing its manpower, Lloyd received an early discharge and enrolled at the University of Nebraska at Lincoln. Although he received a $66-

a-month stipend from the GI Bill and $40 a month from a football scholarship, he still had to work his way through school. At one time, he roomed with 15 other football players, including Lavern Bush, an All-State player from Boys Town.

"Bush and I would go to school, practice football, then work at the railroad yard at night loading box cars," Lloyd recalled. "Bush would go to work in a bakery after that. We usually ate once a day. We'd buy a loaf of bread and a jar of peanut butter every day."

A knee injury forced Bucher to quit football, but he continued to do well in school, working toward a degree in teaching, with minors in geology, chemistry, and mathematics. At about the same time, Father Flanagan died in Germany while on a mission to help children orphaned by the war.

On June 10, 1950, Bucher married his college sweetheart, Rose Roling. Two weeks later, North Korea invaded South Korea and he was called back into the Navy as American forces were beefed up for deployment to the war zone.

But before he could be placed on active duty, Bucher was granted an extension that would allow him to finish school. The tradeoff was that he would enter an officer training program after graduation.

Three years later, with a college degree and a growing family (son Mark was born in 1952), Bucher received his commission as an ensign and was assigned to the USS Mt. McKinley.

Another son, Michael, was born in 1954. A year later, Bucher was accepted for submarine officer training school. For about the next 10 years, he would travel the world aboard submarines, filling various posts on the USS Besugo, the USS Caiman, and the USS Ronquil.

In 1958, Bucher was invited to speak at the Boys Town Athletic Awards Banquet by Monsignor Nicholas Wegner. Wegner had been named Boys Town's executive director after Father Flanagan's death.

Bucher, now a lieutenant on a submarine, was surprised by the invitation but graciously accepted. He hadn't been back to Boys Town for years and he looked forward to seeing the Home again. Bucher later learned that Skip Palrang had lined him up as the banquet speaker and that Monsignor Wegner had arranged the military travel orders that allowed him to fly to Omaha.

"I had never met Monsignor Wegner," Bucher said. "Over the years, we developed a real friendship."

When Bucher had joined the Navy in 1945, he had not intended to make the military his career. But he had developed a love for the sea as a boy living near the Pacific Ocean with his grandparents. As he continued to move up through the ranks, there was no doubt that he had found his calling.

On a winter day in 1966, Bucher learned that he was being reassigned from submarine duty to take command of a newly recommissioned ship, the USS *Pueblo*. The ship was one of a number of Navy auxiliary vessels that were being outfitted for electronic and radio intelligence-gathering missions along the coastlines of Cold War enemies such as the Soviet Union and North Korea. The Soviet Union had been conducting surveillance of U.S. naval forces for years using unarmed fishing trawlers, and these missions were part of the United States response.

At the same time, the war in Vietnam was escalating as the United States continued to send more men and equipment to bolster the sagging South Vietnamese army. Tension was high throughout Asia, as the Communist nations of the region closed ranks against what they perceived as a threat from the West.

Bucher was stationed in Japan with the 7th Fleet as an Assistant Operations Officer for Submarine Flotilla Seven when he was ordered to report to the Navy port in Bremerton, Washington, to assume command of the *Pueblo*. Rose and the boys, who had been living in Japan, flew there with him.

The ship was commissioned on May 13, 1967. Bucher officially took command in a ceremony attended by his wife and Monsignor Wegner.

Over the next few months, the ship's crew trained (for its first mission) and prepared the *Pueblo* for sea duty. The crew of 83 — larger than normal for this size of ship — included 34 electronic communications experts and two Marines who would interpret and decipher radio transmissions. The men were relatively young, with an average age of about 20.

After a number of equipment and technical delays, the ship passed its final inspection, and in November sailed out of San Diego for its home port of Yokosuka, Japan. The ship reached Yokosuka on December 1 after a stormy Pacific crossing. Maintenance on the engines, steering, and some of the sensitive electronic listening gear the ship carried was completed over the next few weeks.

On New Year's Day, 1968, Bucher celebrated his promotion to commander. Four days later, the *Pueblo* left port to cruise to Sasebo, on the southwestern coast of Japan. From there, it would head north into the Sea of Japan to begin its surveillance mission along the coast of North Korea.

The *Pueblo* was 179 feet long and displaced 970 tons. Classified as a light cargo ship before being outfitted for reconnaissance and surveillance, it was small for an ocean-going vessel and offered cramped living quarters for the 83 men aboard. Its top speed was about 13 knots.

Because of the nonaggressive nature of its mission, the *Pueblo* was neither armed nor armor-plated, as a warship would be. The *Pueblo*'s basic protection would stem from the historic right of free passage of ships on the high seas. United States military officials also believed that since the Soviet Union had been using unarmed trawlers to conduct electronic eavesdropping along the periphery of the United States and other Free World nations, the Soviets would not seriously interfere with similar

American efforts. Thus, a *quid pro quo* was deemed to exist. It was further assumed that the Soviets would keep other Communist countries in line with this policy.

In order to provide additional "cover" for the *Pueblo's* mission, two civilian oceanographers and their associated equipment were on board to conduct hydrographic and oceanographic research.

Just one week before the *Pueblo* sailed, though, the Navy Department, in response to an attack on another American surveillance ship, ordered that the *Pueblo* be provided with two .50-caliber machine guns, which Bucher subsequently had mounted in the bow and stern. Bucher planned to train some of his crew to operate the guns while enroute to the waters off North Korea. But inclement weather and heavy seas allowed only a minimum of such training. The cold, snowy weather the *Pueblo* encountered also left a thick coating of ice on the tarps that protected the guns. To get to them, the ice had to be chopped off, a time-consuming chore.

In receiving his orders, Bucher was told that he might expect some harassment from the North Koreans during the mission — it had happened to other American intelligence-gathering ships — but that the risk of attack was minimal. He was assured that if an attack did occur and his ship was in danger, U.S. naval and air forces would be immediately dispatched to come to his aid.

January 23 dawned clear and cold, a sharp contrast to the gale force winds and rough seas that had buffeted the *Pueblo* through most of its voyage. Bucher was happy to see a calm day for a change; many of the men had been seasick and an absence of pitching, rolling waves would give everyone some welcome relief.

The *Pueblo* was lying dead in the water, east of the North Korean port of Wonsan. Bucher had ordered the *Pueblo* to a position about 15 miles east of a small island, located about 25 miles

off the North Korean coast. After the move, he continued to
have his navigator monitor the ship's position.

At 11:30 a.m., the lookouts spotted the first North Korean
ship, a Chinese-built SO-1 submarine chaser.

As the subchaser closed to a thousand yards, Bucher could
see that the vessel's twin 57 millimeter cannon were manned and
aimed at the *Pueblo*. The ship hoisted a flag signal asking what
nationality Bucher's ship was. He responded by having the
American flag raised.

About this time, Bucher ordered a priority message about
the developing situation sent to the Navy high command.

As the subchaser continued to close and started to circle,
another lookout spotted three North Korean patrol boats rapidly approaching from the direction of Wonsan harbor. Now
Bucher again had the *Pueblo*'s position checked. Radar fixes
showed that the American ship was 15.8 miles from the nearest
land, 3.8 miles outside the 12-mile limit.

The four North Korean ships circled the *Pueblo*, while the
subchaser raised another flag signal: "Heave to or I will fire."

Suddenly two North Korean MiG fighter jets made a low
pass over the *Pueblo*. Then another subchaser and another torpedo boat were spotted making their way toward the American
ship.

A short time later, the *Pueblo* was boxed in by six enemy
vessels and two armed aircraft were flying cover.

Bucher earlier had ordered the *Pueblo*'s engines started so
that he could get underway quickly if necessary. Now he ordered
the pilot and engine room to head for the open sea at one-third
speed. He was not going to run, but decided the time had come
to make an orderly withdrawal.

As the *Pueblo* maneuvered and began to pick up speed, the
air was suddenly filled with the sound of gunfire — the first subchaser had opened up with its cannon!

Bucher and the other men on the flying bridge threw

themselves down as the shells raked the radar masts and anten-
nas overhead. Hot pieces of shrapnel cut the air and Bucher felt
searing pain in his legs and buttocks as something cut into his
backside.

As anger overcame his pain, Bucher heard another sound
— the torpedo boats were machine-gunning the *Pueblo*'s decks.
After five or six seconds, the shooting stopped and Bucher asked
the men around him if anyone was hurt. He saw that several men
on the bridge had been hit by shrapnel but no one appeared to
be seriously injured.

Bucher ordered another message sent to Navy high command, this time saying that the *Pueblo* was under fire and that he
had ordered the crew to destroy all classified materials. For the
next hour, the crew would smash, burn, tear, rip, or throw overboard everything they could in order to keep sensitive documents and equipment out of the North Koreans' hands. The
men even set fires in trash cans and began to dump in files and
other documents. Soon, smoke began to fill the ship.

After the North Korean ships unleashed a second burst of
cannon and machine-gun fire, Bucher reached the pilothouse
and ordered new radio messages sent alerting the Navy high
command that the *Pueblo* was still under fire and that crew members had been wounded.

Below decks, one cannon shell hit Fireman Duane Hodges
and exploded in his groin. Hodges, who had been in a passage-
way carrying documents to be destroyed, would die a short time
later. Seventeen other men would be wounded before the firing
stopped.

Finally, the subchaser ordered the *Pueblo* to stop. As the
Pueblo slowed, the gunners on the North Korean boats kept their
weapons trained on the American ship. One of the torpedo boats
swung in close and eight or ten Koreans, led by two officers,
boarded the ship. One of the officers walked straight to Bucher
and pointed a pistol at his face.

Despite Bucher's protests, the Koreans soon were swarming over the ship. The crewmen were bound, blindfolded, and herded together on the fantail.

Bucher was ordered to lead the officers through the ship. Whenever he made a protest or refused to follow their commands to show them how something worked, an officer struck him on the head with a pistol barrel. Anytime he tried to talk to a crewman, both he and the crewman were kicked or received a karate chop across the back of the neck. It was during this time that Bucher learned from a corpsman that Hodges had died.

Bucher was still hopeful that help was on the way. Before the Koreans boarded the *Pueblo*, he had managed to get one last message out. The response indicated that someone in command was trying to scramble Air Force fighter-bombers to the area. But hope began to fade as a North Korean took the helm, pushed the engines to full speed, and headed toward the coastline.

It was late afternoon and already dark when the small convoy reached Wonsan harbor. After the *Pueblo* had docked, the bound, blindfolded crewmen were prodded off the ship at gunpoint and led to waiting buses. A crowd of civilians gathered near the buses, taunting and spitting at the Americans as they walked by.

Bucher was separated from the men and taken before a colonel and a general for interrogation. They accused him and his crew of being CIA spies, and told him they would be tried and shot. Before being placed on a bus, Bucher was taken back onto the *Pueblo* briefly to unlock the door to a room where some of the electronic monitoring equipment was stored. When he refused, he was beaten, and his hands were tied so tightly together that the circulation was cut off.

While the North Koreans did not hesitate to punch or kick any crew member for any reason, they initially singled out a few men who were of Hispanic or Filipino descent for especially brutal beatings. Bucher would later learn that this treatment stemmed from the reason the North Koreans attacked the *Pueblo*.

Two days before the *Pueblo* was seized, North Korean infiltrators had made an unsuccessful attempt to assassinate South Korea's President Park. Bucher was not informed of this incident in the daily news dispatches that were radioed to his ship, so he had no idea that the two countries were on heightened military alert.

Apparently, the North Koreans believed that the *Pueblo*, which had been in the South Korean Navy before being recommissioned, was part of a plot to retaliate by landing a South Korean assassination team in North Korea. After the capture, the North Koreans singled out crew members with Asian features because they were thought to be South Korean spies. That's why those men initially received some of the most severe beatings.

For some time after he was taken off the *Pueblo*, Bucher was subjected to a series of lengthy interrogations. The North Korean officers wanted him to confess to being a CIA spy, and repeatedly threatened him and his crew with execution. Bucher protested that the *Pueblo* was not a spy ship, that it had been on a peaceful oceanographic mission, and that his men were entitled to humane treatment under the Geneva Convention.

But the North Koreans scoffed, punctuating their insistence on a confession with slaps, punches, and kicks. The Americans had no rights, the officers told Bucher, because the United States and North Korea were not at war and because they were being held as spies.

Finally, Bucher and his crew were taken to a train depot and placed on a train. Blindfolded, with hands tightly bound, the men were not allowed to talk during the long ride, which ended early the next morning in the North Korean capital of Pyongyang. Before being let off the train, the blindfolds and bindings were removed. When the men stepped off the train onto the platform, they were blinded by dozens of flashbulbs and movie camera lights. These photos and newsreels would be the first of many that would fuel the North Korean propaganda machine. For months to come, the North Koreans would strictly control what the outside world knew about the *Pueblo* and its crew.

A short time later, Bucher and his men were taken to their first prison, a cluster of small cells whose windows had been boarded up so no light could enter. There, they were issued uniforms and the officers were separated from the enlisted men.

The cells were cold and dirty, and furnished only with a hard cot. Bucher and his officers were kept in solitary confinement, away from the crew. The only time he had contact with them was when a crewman would call to him as he walked down a hallway to the latrine they all shared.

For the men who had been wounded in the attack, pain was a constant companion. Some men stuffed socks into their wounds to stop the bleeding. Infection quickly set in. (A doctor and nurse began providing medical treatment a week later. One seriously wounded crewman underwent surgery in a hospital outside the prison.)

"They expected the United States to retaliate and they were going to execute us all," Bucher would say later. "Not treating the wounded just saved them time and bother."

During their first few days in the prison, the prisoners were frequently beaten and tortured by their captors. When Bucher was being interrogated, he could hear the screams and moans of his men as they were pummeled by the guards. This type of physical abuse would occur often during the men's captivity; many suffered broken jaws, broken ribs, and internal injuries. More than once when Bucher and others used the latrine after beatings, they urinated blood.

It was clear from the first day that the North Koreans would use whatever force was necessary to get Bucher to sign a confession that said the *Pueblo* was illegally spying. With that "proof," they could condemn the United States as the aggressor.

Soon after their arrival at the prison, Bucher was taken into a room for a private session with a colonel he came to refer to as "Super-C" — Super Colonel. At first Super-C was almost pleasant, trying to cajole his prisoner into signing a confession. But when Bucher did not comply, the officer flew into a rage. On the colonel's order, Bucher was beaten so badly that he passed out. When he regained consciousness, he was propped up in a chair and again ordered to sign the confession. Again he refused, and for the second time was beaten into unconsciousness.

When he came to this time, the colonel screamed that if Bucher did not sign in two minutes, he would be shot. Two subordinates yanked Bucher off his chair and made him kneel on the hard floor. One drew his automatic pistol, pointed it at Bucher's head, and turned to the colonel.

This was it. The bluffing was over. Bucher prepared for death, his thoughts on his wife and sons as he waited for the explosion of the gun at his temple. Then the colonel yelled, "Kill the son of a bitch!"

The officer squeezed the trigger. There was only a loud metallic click. A misfire, the colonel said. He told the officer to try again. When the pistol was cocked, no spent shell was ejected. Only then did Bucher realize that the gun wasn't loaded.

"He's not worth the bullet," the colonel said. For a third time, Bucher was kicked and punched like a rag doll, this time more viciously than before. He passed out again and was dragged back to his cell.

A short time later, Bucher was taken to another prison. There, in a dark, dank room, his captors showed him a prisoner they identified as a South Korean spy. The man was hanging from a wall by a leather strap. He had been beaten so badly that one eye protruded from its socket and bruises covered his body. The man had bitten through his bottom lip, and blood caked his face. Bucher could see the man was near death.

This is what happens to spies, the North Koreans told him.

Bucher was sickened by the sight of the dying prisoner. But when he was taken back to his prison and ordered to sign the confession, he again refused. In a rage, Super-C threatened to bring the *Pueblo's* crew into the interrogation cell one by one and shoot each man in front of Bucher, starting with the youngest. The colonel told Bucher that even if he still refused to sign, his crew would be dead and he would eventually give in anyway. Then the colonel ordered the guards to bring in the first prisoner.

Now Bucher couldn't afford to call the colonel's bluff. Afraid for his men, Bucher agreed to sign. He knew the confession was a lie, but he felt that giving the North Koreans what they wanted was the only way to keep his men alive.

When Bucher was taken back to his cell, he found a tray of warm milk, cookies, apple, and boiled eggs. He wanted to eat, but he couldn't.

In the days and weeks that followed, the North Koreans increasingly used Bucher for propaganda activities — scripted press conferences for North Korean "journalists," and interrogation sessions during which they berated his role as a spy for the "warmongering" United States.

One of their high points was the proud announcement to the world that Bucher and his crew had confessed to illegally spying on North Korea. They condemned the United States, ignoring the fact that they had attacked the *Pueblo* while it was in international waters.

At the same time, the North Koreans staged events to support their statements that Bucher and his men were being treated well. The commander was filmed and photographed taking a hot bath and eating a sumptuous meal. But when the cameras were turned off, it was back to the same bleak cell and same bland diet.

Bucher would say later that the North Koreans seemed more interested in propaganda than in any of the materials or

Navy communications specialists they seized with the *Pueblo*.

The propaganda value of the *Pueblo* and its crew played a big role in the negotiations the United States and North Korea were carrying on for the crew's release. The North Koreans stubbornly insisted that the *Pueblo* was spying in their territorial waters, that the *Pueblo* fired the first shots, and that the United States had to admit its guilt before the crew could be released.

Despite strongly worded threats from the United States and demands for the return of the *Pueblo* and its crew, the North Koreans refused to budge. They also warned that they were prepared to go to war should the United States try to use military force to free the crew or retaliate for the *Pueblo*'s capture. All the while, the North Korean negotiators insisted that all of their captives were being treated well.

As the weeks turned into months, Bucher and his men were wearing down physically and mentally. Between the brutal beatings and threats, being isolated from his men, and having given in to his captors, Bucher felt a sense of loneliness and depression that he could not overcome. He had lost all track of time, not knowing whether it was day or night, or how long they had been held captive. At one low point, he considered suicide.

After three months in the prison, the *Pueblo* crew was placed on a train and transported to a second prison camp. Things were a little bit better there. The windows were not boarded up, and three to five men were now housed together in a cell. They also enjoyed 20 to 40 minutes of exercise time each day. But officers were still kept in solitary most of the time, and the physical and mental torture continued.

The conditions were made worse by the terrible food the men had to eat. For almost their whole time in captivity, the *Pueblo* crew lived on a diet of turnips — either cooked in a weak soup or fried in what tasted like rancid butter — and an occasional apple or boiled egg. (Toward the end of their imprisonment, they did receive some black bread.)

Then there was the "salad."

"After cutting the grass, the soldiers would put it on our plates," Bucher recalled. "It was supposed to be a big treat for us, but grass doesn't digest very well in the human stomach."

Without proper food, many of the men came down with scurvy. Others suffered damage to the optic nerve due to a lack of vitamins. Everyone lost weight, and the uniforms that had been issued to the men after their capture hung loosely on thin, starved bodies.

Even when they received something good like apples, the men had to protect their share from the guards. If the men received two apples, they usually would eat one and save one for later. But the guards would search the cells while the men were outside and take the extra apple for themselves.

Bucher's men used these thefts to win a small victory over their captors.

"The next time a guy got an apple he would poke holes in it and urinate on it. Sure enough, a guard took one of those apples, ate it, and got sick. We never saw him (the guard) again."

These small victories became important to morale. From the start, Bucher and his men learned that open defiance or fighting back would only earn a person a good beating. So the officers and crewmen had resorted to more subtle means of resistance. For instance, a crewman might answer a guard's question with an unflattering or derogatory phrase the North Korean didn't understand. One could get away with calling the guards names if it was done cleverly and discreetly. Another favorite way to resist was giving someone "the finger." When the North Koreans asked for an explanation, the crew members told them it was the Hawaiian Good Luck Sign.

While these pranks did help the men keep their spirits up and maintain a sense of humor, the Americans had to be careful. They were always in danger of being tortured and beaten if the North Koreans caught on.

One morale booster the North Koreans had complete con-trol over was the mail being sent to Bucher and his crew from the United States. Although letters from home had begun arriving in North Korea shortly after the *Pueblo* was captured, none of them were given to the crew for seven months. Even then, the North Koreans were selective about who got letters — they often would let one man have mail and withhold it from another. It was another cruel way to damage morale and create jealousies and animosity among the men.

Bucher received three letters from home during the time he was a prisoner. Many more that were written by Rose and others never reached him, but those precious pieces of paper that did were like a godsend.

Rose had been busy writing other letters, too. Working with the families and friends of the other crewmen, she cam-paigned to keep public attention on the *Pueblo* and to push for more action in the efforts to get the crew released. She wrote let-ters to the Navy, the Department of Defense, and any other gov-ernment official that might be able to help. "Remember the *Pueblo*" became the rallying cry for her group and others that sprang up to support Bucher and his men.

Monsignor Wegner also pitched in, pushing for action in letters to President Johnson and the State Department.

Bucher somehow knew Boys Town was looking out for him. Alone in his cell, he often thought about the football trips, the friends he made, and the family he was part of there. On some of the worst days, those memories still could make him smile.

As the summer of 1968 dragged by, it was becoming more difficult for Bucher and his men to endure the malnutrition, lack of medical treatment, and continued physical and mental abuse. Worse, the North Koreans would from time to time hint to Bucher or his officers that the crew would soon be released. But their hopes would be dashed as the deadline came and went.

While those disappointments were painful, the constant

threats of execution were terrifying. Several times, Bucher was taken before a tribunal of army generals who told him he and his crew would be shot for their crimes. Once, Bucher told the North Koreans to shoot him and let his crew and ship go. But the generals and colonels only laughed, saying the ship belonged to them now.

Although he was isolated in his cell most of the time, Bucher managed to talk to his men when he was left alone or when a guard wasn't watching. He and his officers tried to maintain a chain of command and set up a crude system for passing along information to the men. Conversations weren't allowed, but during exercise periods Bucher would try to sneak in an encouraging word or gesture to crew members. During the day, his cell door was kept open, so he could see anyone who passed by. All of this helped Bucher maintain some semblance of command and served as a way to keep track of the men and keep up morale.

In September, the North Koreans made another demand. They wanted Bucher to write a complete and "final" confession about the *Pueblo*'s "spy" mission and all the training he had received for it. Bucher complied with a 40-page document that mixed the North Koreans' twisted facts — what they wanted to hear — and some of the most outlandish and silly statements he could think of ("...and I was briefed in Hawaii by the notorious Marine General Barney Google" [a comic strip character]).

The North Koreans, apparently unaware of the nonsense phrases and references, later filmed Bucher reading the "confession." Then, obviously pleased with his performance, they began to treat the Americans better. Indiscriminate beatings ceased, food became more plentiful, and the demeanor of the guards and officers was more pleasant. In the weeks that followed, the crew even was taken on a series of outings to see a movie, a performance by acrobats and singers, and a war museum.

But in late November, the good treatment stopped. The

North Koreans apparently had caught on to some of the tricks the Americans had been playing on them. What the North Koreans referred to as the "insincerity" of their prisoners would now be punished.

At first, some men were singled out for beatings and privileges were withdrawn. Then on December 11, what became known as Hell Week began.

The main impetus of Hell Week was a propaganda photograph that had been taken earlier of a group of crewmen horsing around in their cell. The men were smiling, and the photo was to be used to show that the Americans were in good spirits.

But several men also could be seen prominently displaying the Hawaiian Good Luck Sign — "giving the finger" — for the camera. Unfortunately, the photo was released to outside news agencies and appeared in *Time* magazine, which in its accompanying story, explained the meaning of the gesture. When the North Koreans saw the magazine and learned they had been tricked, they responded by beating crewmen with sticks, slamming them against walls, and kicking and punching them into unconsciousness. The men also were told that they would be tried and shot.

When Bucher told his captors that he had instigated the gesture and encouraged his men to use it, he was beaten senseless. As he lay on his cot afterwards, he could hear the screams and moans of his men as they were tortured.

Hell Week went on for 10 days. Suddenly, though, the beatings stopped. The North Korean general in charge restored all privileges, and a doctor and nurse began treating the men for their injuries. The men even got some meat with a meal, the first time that had happened since they were captured.

On December 22, Bucher and his men were issued clean uniforms and ordered to assemble in a meeting hall. There, a North Korean officer told them that the United States had agreed to the conditions of their release and had admitted that the *Pueblo* had been illegally spying on North Korea. (A document the United States negotiators had signed included a disclaimer that said everything in the document was a lie and that the United States was signing it only to win the release of the *Pueblo* crew. The North Koreans removed the disclaimer before publicly releasing the document. The United States negotiators also verbally disclaimed the document after signing it.)

The next day, the men were loaded on buses and driven to a train station. They boarded a train, rode several hours, got off the train, and boarded three other buses. A short time later, they arrived at Panmunjon, on the Demilitarized Zone at the border between North and South Korea. This is where American negotiators had worked for months to gain the release of the crew.

Bucher was ordered off his bus and taken to an ambulance. A coffin was opened and an officer asked him to identify the body in it — the body of Duane Hodges, who had been killed when the *Pueblo* was attacked. Bucher did so, then was taken to a building near a foot bridge that crosses the border.

For the next 45 minutes, Bucher stood in the snow and cold as a North Korean officer yelled at him. His feet were freezing in the flimsy tennis shoes he was wearing, and the wind stung his face and hands.

Bucher couldn't understand a word of what the officer was saying. He tried to look like he was paying attention, but all he could think of was that long foot bridge and the 81 men who were sitting in the buses a short distance away.

Bucher tried to forget the pain in his feet as an interpreter stepped forward to tell him what the officer had said. In 30 seconds, he summed up the officer's tirade: Bucher had been condemned to death as an enemy of the people of North Korea.

Then, abruptly, the interpreter said: "Now get out of here and don't come back or you'll be shot on sight."

The words didn't immediately register. After 11 months in captivity, with countless promises of release that were never kept, he couldn't believe that this could be it. Not wanting to give the Koreans a chance to change their minds, Bucher tried to walk away. But his frozen feet wouldn't move. Finally, painfully, he took a few faltering steps toward the bridge.

He crossed the bridge with strides that became quicker as he neared the other side. Army and Navy officers were waiting to welcome him. The body of crewman Hodges was carried over. Then Bucher turned to watch and account for his crew as they crossed the bridge one by one.

It was December 23, 1968. After 336 days in captivity, the crew of the USS Pueblo was free.

The realization that he was finally free didn't hit Bucher until he had been escorted to a reception building.

"I was provided the best banquet I've ever attended," he said. "I got a cup of coffee and a doughnut. It was like coming back from the grave."

Over the next few hours, Bucher and his men were debriefed and treated for injuries at an Army hospital. Bucher appeared at a press conference to answer questions. That night in the hospital he arranged for the crew to have a brandy eggnog in celebration of their return.

The next day — Christmas Eve — they boarded C-141 transport planes and flew to Mirimar Naval Air Base in San Diego, California.

Neither Bucher nor his men were prepared for the welcome they received as they got off the plane. Hundreds of family members, friends, naval personnel, and reporters were waiting, waving and cheering. The band was playing "The Lonely Bull," the Pueblo's theme song.

Bucher was greeted by a vice admiral. Then he walked down the steps to the tarmac, and almost ran to the waiting arms of Rose and his sons.

That night, the reunited Bucher family spent Christmas Eve together.

In the months that followed, Bucher would require frequent hospitalization and at least one operation for the wounds and injuries he suffered. His weight had dropped from 200 to 127 pounds during his captivity, and it would be some time before he regained his physical health.

By his own admission, Bucher was "a nervous and emotional wreck." The months of solitary confinement and torture had taken their toll and he was placed on limited duty while he recovered.

In February 1970 at a Court of Inquiry, a still-frail Bucher recounted the *Pueblo*'s capture and the torturous 11 months of captivity that followed. After hearing other testimony, the Court recommended that Bucher and some of his officers be court-martialed for surrendering their ship without a fight and for allowing the North Koreans to capture sensitive documents. This recommendation was made despite evidence that suggested that the *Pueblo* was ill-equipped to defend itself or to destroy the documents it carried.

Secretary of the Navy John H. Chafee decided later, however, that all charges should be dropped, saying of the *Pueblo* crew, "They have all suffered enough."

In a statement explaining his decision, Chafee wrote:

"Commander Bucher upheld morale in a superior manner; that he provided leadership by insisting that command structure be maintained and providing guidance for conduct; and that he contributed to the ability of the crew to hold together and withstand the trials of detention until repatriation could be effected."

Rear Admiral Edward Rosenberg recommended Bucher for the nation's highest military award, the Medal of Honor, but final approval was withheld. However, Bucher and the other men who were wounded received the Purple Heart. Later the entire crew received the Combat Action Ribbon for actions during the attack and the Purple Heart for abuses suffered in captivity.

On Bucher's recommendation, medals were awarded to some of his officers and men for bravery under fire or exemplary performance during captivity. Those awards included the Navy Cross, the Silver Star, the Bronze Star, and the Navy Commendation Medal.

If there was any question about how the crewmen of the *Pueblo* felt about their commander, it was answered in a message sent to him during the Court of Inquiry:

> Dear Captain,
>   We've made it this far together, and we'll finish it together.
>
>   Bucher's Bastards

In the end, Bucher remained in the Navy and eventually was assigned as Chief Staff Officer to a flotilla that participated in the mining and de-mining of Haiphong harbor as part of the military effort against North Vietnam. The debate over what would be known as "the *Pueblo* incident" would continue for years.

In April 1970, Bucher and his wife accepted Monsignor Wegner's invitation to a homecoming celebration at Boys Town.

The Buchers arrived in Omaha the night before the banquet. As they got off their plane, a large group of young boys began hollering, waving American flags, and holding up signs and banners. As he got closer, Bucher could see they were from Boys Town.

"Father Wegner had bused all the kids from Boys Town out to the airport to welcome me," Bucher recalled. "The band was playing and all the kids were standing along the fence. I was in tears. I couldn't believe it."

Bucher walked along the fence, smiling and shaking hands. Then he and Rose rode in a 50-vehicle motorcade through downtown Omaha on their way to Boys Town. It was the first day of "Bucher Days."

The next night, nearly 1,200 people gathered for a banquet in the Boys Town Fieldhouse. Among the guests were U.S. senators, the governor, Boys Town football coach Skip Palrang, some members of the *Pueblo* crew, and all of the Boys Town kids.

In his speech, Bucher paid tribute to his crew for their support and told the crowd that the prayers of the American people had sustained them during their captivity. He concluded by saying: "From the depth of my soul and the bottom of my heart I thank each and every one of you for honoring me this evening. It has been the most glorious day of my life."

For several years after his release, Bucher's celebrity followed him wherever he went. His picture and story appeared in countless magazines and newspapers, and television cameras often intruded on his Navy and private life.

In January 1973, Bucher was told that he was being assigned to a desk job. For someone whose love of the Navy stemmed from his love of the sea, that was enough of a reason to retire. So after 27 1/2 years in the service of his country, Bucher left the Navy and started a new life.

Having completed his autobiography, *Bucher: My Story*, in 1970, he tried his hand at writing novels, then developed an interest in painting. After some time of self-instruction, he submitted a portfolio to the Art Center of Design in Pasadena. He was accepted, and used his experience to embark on a career as an artist, painting on commission.

Today, Lloyd and Rose Bucher live a quiet life in Poway, California. His painting keeps him busy, and he occasionally speaks before groups and organizations, something he's been doing since the 1970s.

Bucher's bond with Boys Town remains strong. His black leather Navy jacket with the *USS Pueblo* emblem is on display at the Home's Hall of History, just a few steps from Bucher Drive, the campus street named for him.

"That's about as close to family as I've ever had," Bucher says of Boys Town.

In the years that have passed since the *Pueblo's* capture, Bucher also has continued to keep in touch with his other family – the men of the *Pueblo* who shared his harrowing ordeal. *The Lonely Bull*, a newsletter for former *Pueblo* crew members, is published quarterly. In 1986, the crew had its first reunion and now gathers every three years.

In 1990, 22 years after the *Pueblo's* capture, Bucher and his crew were recognized as having been prisoners of war and received POW medals.

"There's still a strong bond between the men," Bucher said. "Those kinds of experiences create strong bonds. We get together to celebrate survival as well as friendship."

Persian Gulf War

Boys Town, as much as any other small village or town across the country, felt the impact of the war triggered by Iraq's invasion of Kuwait in August 1990.

By the time the war ended with an Allied victory the following February, more than 30 former Boys Town residents were on active duty in the Persian Gulf region.

Many were recent graduates, young people who had friends and teachers at Boys Town. Some had been in the service or reserve units for years. Most saw the war up close. They were members of frontline units and rear support companies. They were sailors on warships that cruised the gulf coast, providing naval bombardment and protecting ground troops.

The reality of war and the possibility of death in a foreign land tested the faith of many of those who joined the service after leaving Boys Town. Fortunately, every one who served in the Gulf war came home safely.

On the home front, Father Val J. Peter, Boys Town's executive director since 1985, organized a letter-writing campaign to provide support for the soldiers overseas.

Boys Town school children wrote countless letters to former residents who were overseas. A Christmas tree bearing tags with the names of all of the Boys Town alumni serving in the Persian Gulf was erected in Dowd Chapel. When a soldier returned home safely, his name was taken off the tree. The tree remained up until everyone came home.

The bonds between Boys Town and its former citizens were strengthened or renewed many times throughout the war. Many changes had occurred at Boys Town since the Vietnam War — girls were admitted starting in 1979 and more services were developed and offered to families and parents outside the Home — but the feeling of belonging never changed for former residents. Messages of hope and encouragement from the troops at the front served as a source of inspiration for many of the kids back at Boys Town.

As one former Boys Town youth stationed in the Persian Gulf said in a note to the children: "Stand tall and be proud. You are from Boys Town."

Desert victory

When Iraqi dictator Saddam Hussein unleashed his powerful army on the tiny nation of Kuwait on Aug. 2, 1990, the shock wave was felt around the world.

After easily crushing the Kuwaiti army, Iraq began to mass thousands of troops, tanks, and artillery pieces on the Saudi Arabian border. Hussein proclaimed that Kuwait was now part of Iraq, and warned that any attempt to challenge the invasion would lead to a bloody and costly war for the United States and its allies.

The United States and United Nations Security Council immediately condemned the invasion and demanded the withdrawal of Iraqi troops. President George Bush signed orders banning trade with Iraq and freezing Iraq's and Kuwait's assets in the United States. And the United States and its allies pledged to protect other nations that were being threatened by the Iraqis.

Five days after the invasion, President Bush received permission from Saudi Arabia's King Fahd to deploy U.S. forces on Saudi soil. U.S. combat units began leaving for the Persian Gulf.

In the weeks that followed, Bush and other world leaders fashioned a 28-nation coalition that eventually would build a fighting force numbering nearly one million, including 540,000 American troops.

Thus began a six-month faceoff in the desert, a faceoff that would end in a dramatic military victory for coalition forces and freedom for Kuwait.

Ron Dennis, Ron Nichols, Ray Huckeby, Ron McKamy, and nearly 40 other Boys Town alumni were among those American forces that helped restore Kuwait's independence and thwart Hussein's quest for power. Some were young, recent graduates who had joined the military right out of high school. Others were older — career soldiers, Army reservists, or members of National Guard units.

For all of them, even the few who had seen combat in Vietnam, the idea of going to war was a terrifying prospect that required discipline and courage. The real possibility of death on a foreign battlefield tested their faith. And leaving families and friends was one of the hardest things they ever had to do.

This was a new kind of war. It was televised to the people back home. It was a war of high-tech, radar-controlled weapons. It was a long-distance war where battles would be fought by ground forces that could only see each other on radar screens. But like all wars, it was fought by people; people who would bleed and die.

Throughout the Persian Gulf War, the bond between Boys Town and its former "kids" remained strong. Prayers and masses were offered daily for the safety of the troops. School children at Boys Town wrote countless letters to servicemen and servicewomen overseas. A Christmas tree bearing yellow ribbons and tags with the names of all of the Boys Town alumni serving in the Persian Gulf was put up in Dowd Chapel, the Catholic church at Boys Town. When a soldier returned home safely, his or her name was taken off the tree. The tree remained up until all came home.

The Persian Gulf War was a touchstone for the men and women who fought in it. For Ron Dennis, Ron Nichols, Ray Huckeby, Ronald McKamy, and the other Boys Town alumni who were there, it also was a proving ground for the lessons they had learned and the strength of character they had gained at Boys Town.

★ Saying goodbye ★

Pvt. Ron McKamy was preparing for a nightfire exercise on the M-16 range at Fort Campbell, Kentucky, when his unit got the news.

It was Wednesday, August 8. McKamy, an assistant gunner and driver with an artillery battery in 5th Charlie Company, 101st Airborne Division, had graduated from air assault school a day earlier. The school had been tough and McKamy was looking forward to spending some time with his wife and son, who was nearly a year old.

A South Vietnamese orphan who was adopted by an American couple when he was two, McKamy had lived in Nebraska and Texas with his family until he was placed in Boys Town in 1984.

"I was at the rebellious stage and I felt I wasn't happy with life at the time," McKamy said. "I didn't feel that my parents were giving me what I needed. So I ran away when we were living in Fort Worth. I was in trouble with drinking and drugs and depression."

When he graduated from Boys Town in 1988, McKamy wanted to attend college. He took classes at a small community college for a summer, but then started to slide back into his old lifestyle of partying with friends. About this time, McKamy met Raina, who would become his wife in February 1989. McKamy changed, dedicating himself to his relationship with Raina. When the couple learned that Raina was pregnant, McKamy decided to join the Army so that he could support his young family. He enlisted in May and Joshua was born in September.

Now as McKamy and his buddies readied their weapons, an officer came in and told them to gather in the day room. A few minutes later, they were being told that they were going to Saudi Arabia.

"The guys who were married could go home and pack up and be back by five in the morning, ready to ship out," McKamy recalled. "That's all you could tell your family."

McKamy got home late that night. He walked inside, told Raina that he was being sent overseas, and told her how much he loved her and Joshua. Then he said he'd be back and started packing.

"I don't know how she felt at the time, but I know she was hurting. I was hurting, too. We didn't really get to spend much time together. Joshua was born in September of 1989. He was coming up on a year old. It was really hard that I only had one night to stay with Raina. It was a rough night."

The next morning, a friend picked up Ron to take him to his unit's assembly point. As the car pulled away, Raina stood on the porch crying.

Ron spent the day loading equipment and doing maintenance on vehicles and weapons. As the driver of the five-ton truck that pulled his gun crew's 155-millimeter howitzer, he had to make sure they could get where they were going once they touched down in Saudi Arabia. That night, the unit slept in the motor pool garage. Early the next morning, they left for Fort Bragg, North Carolina, where they spent two weeks before finally flying to Dhahran in Saudi Arabia aboard a commercial airliner.

"We were one of the first units to come in," McKamy recalled. "We stayed in Dhahran for about two weeks at a Saudi National Guard base waiting for the rest of the battalion and our equipment to get there. As soon as our guns and trucks got there, we rolled out.

"The first place we stayed we called 'Scorpion City' because there were so many scorpions. We were camped in the middle of nowhere. We put up nets and tents, and dug foxholes."

It was early September. Joshua's first birthday party was three weeks away and McKamy was going to miss it.

Iraq announced on August 17 that it would "play host" to citizens of the "aggressive nations" that had imposed sanctions on Iraq or were sending troops and ships to the gulf region. On August 18, U.S. warships fired warning shots at two outbound Iraqi tankers.

President Bush ordered a limited mobilization of U.S. military reserves on August 22. The flow of troops and military equipment into the Persian Gulf region increased.

Operation Desert Shield was now in full swing.

Ron Dennis and Ron Nichols had known each other since they were roommates at Boys Town.

Now they were both caught up in the whirlwind of activity that was sweeping through the U.S. Marine base at Twenty-Nine Palms, California.

The rumors had been flying for several days, ever since Iraq's invasion of Kuwait. One had the Marines going to Turkey to protect the Iraq-Turkey border. Both Dennis and Nichols had been involved in mountain terrain training when their units had been told to prepare to move out on short notice. When they were sent to Twenty-Nine Palms in mid-August for desert climatizing, they had a pretty good idea of their ultimate destination.

"That night I was packing my bags and signing a power of attorney document and signing a will," Dennis remembered. "I knew it was getting serious. But I also thought it was a joke because they like to see if they can get everybody together on alerts."

The next time Dennis saw his old Boys Town roommate, he knew it was the real thing.

"Ron (Nichols) was packing an M-249 automatic machine gun. I wasn't ready to go yet and didn't know if it was really going to happen. This guy's got grenades, he's got 2,000 bullets, machine gun, mines, the whole nine yards. They're not issuing this, and you're not signing for it — they're throwing this stuff at you."

Dennis did manage to call Father Val Peter, Boys Town's executive director, the night before he left. He told the priest he was worried, but when the two men said goodbye, Dennis felt better. Then, like hundreds of other Marines, he was on a crowded TWA commercial airliner headed east.

Dennis and his buddies did what they could to relax. But there was little escape from the tension that hung in the air of the cramped passenger cabin.

"There were Marines on the floor. We had machine guns and grenades. I remember a sergeant telling us, 'Make sure your grenades don't hang off your packs. Make sure your grenades are in a secure place. If those pins get pulled, we're in a lot of trouble on this plane.'"

The first stop for Dennis's flight was New York City, where the Marines changed planes. Passengers waiting for flights stared in amazement as several hundred men wearing combat uniforms and carrying machine guns, rifles, and other equipment trudged through the terminal. Then it was on to Belgium, Italy, and finally, Saudi Arabia.

Dennis and Gulf Company 27 touched down in Riyadh on August 19. The blast-furnace desert heat that hit them as they got off the plane would be a constant companion for the next few months.

The unit quickly was set up in quarters in Riyadh and assigned to guard an ammunition dump and a nearby compound that served as headquarters for high-ranking officers.

"The ammo dump was as big as Boys Town," he said. "That was my job, to just walk up and down along this ammo dump. The thing I was really worried about was terrorists."

Security was tight everywhere. Dennis and other guards would confront any unauthorized person or vehicle with their weapons loaded and ready to fire. There were snipers on surrounding buildings and machine guns mounted in towers on the compound perimeter. Marines carrying automatic weapons and wearing goggles to protect their eyes from blowing sand patrolled streets constantly.

When they weren't on guard duty, Dennis and his unit were training. It was not the kind of training that Dennis liked.

"For the first time ever I was being trained to kill people. One of the officers was teaching us what are called 'quick kill' techniques. He said, 'You're not shooting for a two-point takedown. You've got to kill them in the first 45 seconds.' I was thinking, 'Man, just two years ago I was playing basketball at the Boys Town Fieldhouse.'"

Dennis called Father Peter when he could. It bothered him to think that he might have to kill another person and he talked to Father Peter about it. Dennis hoped it would never happen.

Ron Nichols, meanwhile, had flown out of Twenty-Nine Palms on August 15 with Alpha Company of the Seventh Marine Division. When his unit arrived in Saudi Arabia a few days later, it was quartered in converted warehouses because barracks were still under construction.

More men and equipment poured into the area as the days went by. Training continued as company commanders tried to keep their men sharp and work out the logistical nightmare of finding housing for the troops and space for vehicles, weapons, ammunition, food, and other supplies.

"We went out into the desert for weeks at a time," Nichols said. "We would relieve the units guarding the Kuwaiti border. The officers were getting us ready for chemical warfare and how to use the antibiotics. Chemical warfare was one of our main fears."

For the next few months, Dennis and Nichols rotated between a front line post on the Saudi-Iraqi border and a rear area, where they could shower, get their mail, and relax. During those rest periods, Dennis and Nichols often were able to get together and talk, which made being in a war zone a little easier. They weren't being told much but it was clear from the news they heard on the radio and the rumors that flew around the camps that they wouldn't be going home soon.

Ray Huckeby had joined the Army in late 1965, about a year and a half after he graduated from Boys Town. Because he had some experience driving heavy trucks, he was assigned to a transportation company and began light and heavy vehicle training school.

Huckeby had been sent to the Home in 1959 when he was 12. His placement was arranged by a family friend who saw that the boy was running with the wrong crowd and was headed for big trouble. Huckeby fit in well at Boys Town. He would rise at 5 a.m. to work on the farm, then go to school at 7:30 a.m. Classes were sometimes difficult, but Huckeby stuck with his studies and got through school, graduating in 1964. Even more important, he left Boys Town with some valuable lessons about life. The discipline that Huckeby learned at Boys Town served him well in the Army.

In 1966, given a choice of assignments, Huckeby and 20 other men in his unit volunteered to go to Vietnam.

Instead, they were all sent to Germany and Huckeby was made an infantryman. While in Germany, he tried two more times to volunteer for duty in Vietnam. Both requests were denied. Meanwhile, he met and married a German woman.

Huckeby was stationed at Fort Riley in Kansas when his hitch ended in 1968. By this time, he and his wife had a daughter. While on the way back to Tennessee, where Huckeby planned to look for work, the family stopped in Omaha to visit Ray's brother and sister. Then the Huckebys' daughter got pneumonia.

"We took her down to the hospital and they put her in intensive care for a couple of days," Huckeby said. "Then they presented us with this huge hospital bill. We decided to stay for awhile and pay off the bill. We've been here paying off bills ever since."

Huckeby worked at different jobs for a couple of years before being hired as a driver with an over-the-road trucking company. He eventually made his home in Mead, Nebraska, not far from Omaha.

In 1971, he and his brother, Mack, who graduated from Boys Town in 1958, decided to join the Army Reserves as a joke.

"Another former Boys Town boy, Jim Bolita, was first sergeant in a transportation unit. We talked to Jim a couple of times at alumni meetings and he kept trying to convince us to join. We finally decided to go down and join, and then ride Jim about it."

Assigned to the 172nd Transportation Company, Huckeby began driving transports and other vehicles as part of his reserve duties. The transports were used mainly for moving military equipment. Two days a month and two weeks during the summer, he gathered with other reservists to train, learning how to lash cargo to the trailers and how to move it. By 1990, he had earned the rank of staff sergeant.

Huckeby enjoyed the military. He also figured that it was only a matter of time before the United States would be involved in a conflict that might make it necessary to call up reserve units to active duty. He figured there was a good chance that he might still see combat someday.

Then in October 1990, Huckeby picked up a newspaper during a run between Omaha and Denver and read that his reserve outfit had been placed on standby alert because of the crisis in the Persian Gulf. At the time, Huckeby was serving as a motor pool sergeant for a cavalry (scout) squadron. But he wanted to be with his unit if it was going to Saudi Arabia. When he reached Denver, he contacted his unit administrator and asked for a transfer back to the 172nd. The process took less than 30 minutes. Two days later, when he got back home, he told his wife what had happened and began packing his bags.

"Maybe I thought it was going to be a thrill or an adventure," Huckeby said. "I don't really know. I never stopped to question why I did it."

Huckeby's brother, Mack, who was still in the 172nd, also had volunteered to go overseas. He could have stayed home because of a diabetic condition, but chose to go with his unit. In late October, the brothers and their company were sent to Fort Riley, Kansas, for training in convoy tactics and the use of protective suits and gas masks in case of a gas or chemical attack.

On November 6, Huckeby and 324 other soldiers boarded a 747 headed for Saudi Arabia. They were not allowed off the plane for almost 24 hours, not even when the jet landed for fuel or to change crews. The flight touched down at Dhahran in the middle of the night and the weary reservists stepped out into the warm desert air.

Ray Huckeby's adventure had begun.

Other Boys Town alumni were in Saudi Arabia or on their way about the same time. Army Sgt. Josef Gray, a 1983 graduate, got the word at Fort Campbell, Kentucky. Anthony Killila, Class of 1990, was a crewman aboard the USS Missouri, one of the two American battleships sent to the Persian Gulf. First Sgt. John Browers, a 1967 graduate, had seen combat in Vietnam. At 42, he was with a Patriot missile unit, a weapon that would be instrumental in thwarting Iraq's long-range Scud missiles. Sgt. William M. Smith, Class of 1959, also had served in Vietnam. Private Steven Davis, a Marine artilleryman, graduated in 1987.

Throughout the war, they and the others who were in the Middle East would continue or renew their contact with Boys Town through letters and phone calls. From desert sands half a world away, it was like writing or calling home.

★ The buildup ★

By September 1990, planes and ships loaded with troops, weapons, equipment, food, and other supplies were arriving in Saudi Arabia around the clock. A U.S. aircraft carrier battle group that was ordered to the Persian Gulf shortly after the invasion of Kuwait was soon to be joined by two other battle groups. American air forces being sent to the region included American F-15 fighter jets, B-52 bombers, and AWACS radar planes, and 100,000 ground troops, along with heavy artillery and tanks, were already in defensive positions.

At the same time, other nations pledged to provide military or financial support to halt Iraqi aggression.

Meanwhile, Saddam Hussein stubbornly refused to comply with the United Nations' demands that all Iraqi troops be pulled out of Kuwait. Iraq continued to fortify its positions along the Kuwait-Saudi border, and thousands of foreign citizens living in Iraq were detained as hostages.

Ron McKamy held his hands over his ears as the big howitzer blasted its shell over the flat, hot desert. Since arriving at Camp Scorpion, near the Saudi-Kuwaiti border, his battery had participated in firing exercises almost daily. In ground combat, artillery would play a key role in supporting the infantry and knocking out enemy fortifications. It was hot, but to make things worse, the men had to wear gas masks just about everywhere they went. Commanders wanted the men to stay sharp and acclimate themselves to the conditions they would be fighting in.

"It would be 110 to 120 degrees when we were out in the morning," McKamy said. "A lot of people passed out. You can't imagine having that (mask) on your face when it's so hot. But it's a good thing we did it because we finally started getting used to it."

The first few weeks in the desert were hard on McKamy. Like many other soldiers, he had been taken from his family, flown halfway around the world, and then sent into a scorching wasteland where he had to live in a bunker and keep an eye out for scorpions. For security reasons, the men were kept in the dark about what was going on elsewhere and when they could expect to see action. This only added to the daily tension.

"I missed my wife and kid. We were scared because we didn't know what to expect," McKamy recalled. "We didn't have any electricity, no toilets, no showers; we were taking baths out of a bucket. After about a month of that, we started getting used to it. It almost got to where we didn't even think there was a war. Then, about the end of November, we started getting showers and snack bars and phones put in."

About that time, McKamy and his comrades were reminded of where they were and why they were there. On the Sunday after Thanksgiving, McKamy was standing in line in the mess tent, talking to the cooks while waiting to be served a holiday weekend brunch. Suddenly, people were yelling for everyone to get in their bunkers.

"I remember jumping into a foxhole and throwing on a gas mask," McKamy recalled. "Someone said that Iraq had launched a Scud missile. That's when Iraq hit Dhahran. We called it 'Scud Sunday.'"

From that day on, McKamy knew he would soon be shooting back.

Confusion reigned during the first few days Ray Huckeby's

transportation company was in Saudi Arabia. First, the unit had no way to get around because their vehicles and equipment weren't scheduled to arrive for a week. Then no one met them when they landed; the headquarters they were assigned to apparently didn't know the unit had arrived. Finally, no arrangements had been made for the unit's housing.

"We loaded onto buses that were on a 24-hour call and followed a 2 1/2-ton truck that had picked up some late arrivals to a place called Half-Moon Bay," Huckeby recalled. "We were there for three days before our assigned headquarters unit found out where we were. We slept in small tents and even in wooded crates we 'borrowed' from a water purification unit."

Conditions at the company's temporary "camp" were not the best. Blowing sand was a constant nuisance and they had no hot water; the only way to stay halfway clean was to sneak into a supply company's billet late at night and use the showers.

Because it was October — winter in Saudi Arabia — the heat was bearable. Days were warm and nights saw temperatures in the 70s. This was shirt-sleeve weather for the Americans. But not everyone enjoyed the cool nights; Huckeby often would see foreign laborers wearing coats and hats with ear muffs.

When their trucks finally arrived by ship, Huckeby and his men were assigned to take over a water run to the front lines. This meant driving flatbed trucks loaded with a 4,750-gallon water bag over narrow roads from Dhahran to outposts and bases in the desert. The water was used for drinking, bathing, and building roads. The usual routine would be to drive one day, rest one day, complete vehicle maintenance, then start over.

Huckeby's unit knew little of what was going on in the region until it had been in Saudi Arabia for a month. Most of their news came from radio reports, or from scuttlebutt passed along by units that had microwave receivers tuned in to American television news stations. One thing they did know was that more troops were coming in every day, which meant more work for the units that were hauling water to the front.

Eventually, the company moved into its own quarters — a one-story concrete block building on the site of an abandoned trucking company. Then all the mail from home that had been held up because they didn't have permanent housing caught up with them. Huckeby couldn't believe all the letters from kids at Boys Town. As he read each carefully written message, his morale soared. The people back home hadn't forgotten them!

While delivery of drinking water was its main mission, Huckeby's unit also supplied water for roads that engineers were building through the desert. These roads would link the network of outposts and improve travel.

"They have a tremendous interstate system in Saudi Arabia," Huckeby recalled. "Once you get off the interstate, it's a whole different program. There were a lot of dirt roads. When you peel off the top 10 to 15 inches of loose sand and wet it down, you can pack it and it gets just like concrete. For awhile, we were working with a unit that was building roads. They were pushing the sand off and we would haul the water up. They'd put the water in a tanker truck with a sprayer and make a road."

A normal day sometimes involved 10 to 12 hours of driving. Convoys were made up of as few as two or three trucks to as many as 70. Sometimes, a convoy would travel only 150 miles a day if it ran into road construction or bad roads.

Although the convoys passed through "friendly" territory, they sometimes were no more than five or ten miles from the Iraqi border. And there was always the danger of a Scud or gas attack, or an attack by infiltrators or terrorists. But the biggest threat to the convoys was often just around the next curve.

"We liked to say that we were under attack every day by the local drivers," Huckeby said. "We'd only been out for about a week on convoy when a civilian tractor-trailer crossed over and collided with one of our tractor-trailers. One of our guys was severely injured and the co-driver was shaken up. The civilian driver was killed. Civilians were getting killed every day. They didn't understand military convoy procedure. They'd pull out in front of you in a heartbeat."

Huckeby often stood guard with his M-16 rifle while his men unloaded the water from the trucks. (That became the usual routine after he broke his wrist tightening a strap on a water bag and had to have a cast put on.) While driving, the men carried protective suits and everyone was required to have a gas mask with them at all times.

"They told us we could go into town in civilian clothes but you had to carry your gas mask everywhere," Huckeby said. "You didn't want to offend anyone so you'd take your gas mask and put it in a green laundry bag and carry it over your shoulder so the people couldn't see it. They didn't have gas masks."

★ Mail call ★

Even in a war where many soldiers could regularly make phone calls home, the arrival of mail still was the most eagerly awaited event of the day.

Boys Town made sure its former residents in the Persian Gulf got plenty of letters. As part of a massive campaign to boost morale, Boys Town school children, teachers, Family-Teachers, and administrators sent hundreds of cards and notes to the Gulf region. Like any small town, Boys Town came together to take care of its own.

For those at the front, the outpouring of support from their Boys Town family made them feel a little less homesick. It helped to know that people cared and were behind them.

When the former Boys Town "kids" wrote home, those feelings came through in their heartfelt and sometimes poignant words. Amid the news about the hot weather, the boredom, and the ongoing training, there was a sense of pride in who they were and why they were there.

7 Dec. 90

Father Peter,

Thank you so much for your letter. As I
read the reasons some of the students had
for being thankful, I saw a little of me in all
of them. I've spent 30 days already on the
Kuwait border; now I'm at our base camp. I
will return to the border on 15 Dec. We don't
know what to expect, we never have news
that is current, and scorpions are as numerous as spiders in the States.

As I reflect on the time I have already
spent here, living with a sword swinging over
my head, you would think my life wasn't
going so good. Well, I've failed to mention that
through the holidays that I've missed, and
the heat I've had to endure, the precious time
I've missed with my wife and children, and
the possibility of war being so great, there
has been one thing consistent, reliable, and
comforting in my life. And that's Jesus. He is,
and always will be, my light in the dark.

Father Peter, I'm in a no-lose situation.
If God brings me home to the States, I win.
And if God should call me to his almighty
kingdom, I've won also. Father, my message
to the students is this: Hang on to Jesus with
everything you've got, because there may
come a time when there is nothing else to
hold on to. And He will provide.

Thanks again for your concern.

My prayer list will include you.

Sincerely,
Sgt. Josef Gray
Boys Town Class of 1983

Dear Boys Town,

I'd like to begin by just telling you that
there have been many many scared, unsure,
lonely minutes since my graduation.

I never forget Boys Town. Sometimes,
when I'm sitting in my bunker, dug in 30
miles from Kuwait, memories begin to linger.
I find myself running down that football field
or singing "He Ain't Heavy" in my earlier
days with the Boys Town choir.

My dear brothers and sisters, the love
that I feel when receiving your letters and
packages is unexplainable. Like many of you,
throughout my childhood, I suffered emotion-
ally and physically.

My fellow younger brothers and sisters,
look around more often when you walk to
and from school because maybe you'll one
day need those memories to survive the
moment. Pay more attention to the people sitting next to you. They won't always be sitting
there. Most of all, appreciate the lessons of
life at Boys Town. Just like me, one day your
training will be done and you will be expected
to accomplish the mission.

Semper Fidelis,
Ron Dennis

11/16/90

Dear Father Peter,

Hi! How are you doing?

Well, I'm here in Saudi Arabia. I've been
away from home (Fort Campbell, Ky.) now for
three months, almost four. I'm not sure how
long I'm going to be here. I'm scared, but I'll
survive.

I got married February 14, 1989, and I
have a son now. My wife and my son are the
best things that have happened in my life,
Father Peter. I miss them a lot, too. It looks
like we'll be here for Christmas. I'm not
happy about that, but there's nothing I can do
about it.

My morale is low, but I should be OK. I

know I can survive anything as long as my
wife and son are OK, and I have people supporting me. We may not be in combat, but
this takes a lot out of us here. I pray every-
day that we'll be home soon and safe.

Thank you for your support through the
years and please have people write because I
look for mail call every day.

Sincerely,
PFC Ronald McKamy

Dec. 3, 1990
Dear Father Peter,

Well, if you haven't heard by now,
Saddam fired three missiles from Iraq toward
Israel, but they never made it, so we don't
know what was going on. All we knew was
that we were packing our things and getting
ready to go into Kuwait, but we didn't and
now we're just waiting again.

Let me tell you, when we were packing
our things, I sort of felt relieved when we
heard he fired those missiles and we all
thought we were going to fight. But I also felt
scared. I was wondering that if we had gone,
whether I was going to come back.

Sincerely,
Ronald H. Nichols
Boys Town Class of 1988

Jan. 1991
Dear Father Val,

Received your letter last night and was
very pleased to hear from you even though I
know from past experience that the Home
takes watch over its own.

This is certainly a strange, and in many
ways, a beautiful country. A lot has been
made of the laws and customs here concerning the Arab treatment of women. They are
actually very protective of women and pun-

ishment for crimes against females is quick and very severe. As a result, rape and physical abuse are almost never head of. Compare that to our civilized world.

The weather is cooling down and it is supposed to rain tomorrow. That will be a welcome change from the dust and fine sand that seems to be everywhere. I was on a munitions run to the King Khalid Military City on New Year's Day and it got cold enough to freeze water (a rare experience here I'm told).

I've read a lot about how low morale is among some of the units here. Speaking for a lot of the people in the 172nd Trans. Co., "we are here to do a job; let's do it and then we can come home with our heads high." Yes, we may have a few problems and things may not go our way all the time but these people are proud to serve and will survive.

Say hello to all and pray for peace.

Sincerely,
Ray Huckeby

★ A long way from home ★

When he was in seventh grade, Ron Nichols had been given a school assignment to write about what he wanted to be when he grew up. At first, he couldn't come up with any ideas. Then, while watching television, he saw a recruitment commercial for the Marine Corps. His mind was made up then and there: He wanted to be a Marine.

Nichols was living with a foster family in Stockbridge, Michigan, at the time. A judge had ordered the placement after he was taken away from his mother as a youngster. Since his father didn't want him, there was no other place to go.

Nichols loved his foster family. But he was constantly in trouble at home, at school, and on the streets. In April 1986, his foster parents decided they couldn't handle the boy and the courts sent him to Boys Town.

Boys Town gave Nichols a new start. His Family-Teachers helped him learn self-control, and he worked hard to get good grades in school as he made new friends. One of his best friends was Ron Dennis, his roommate.

In 1988, just before graduating from high school, Nichols joined the Marines on a delayed-entrance program. Two days after commencement exercises, he was in boot camp in San Diego, California.

Nichols liked military life. The training was tough, but he knew it would be. By the time he was sent to the Persian Gulf, Nichols was a lance corporal.

As a Marine, Nichols knew that there might come a time when he would have to put what he was learning to use on a battlefield. But the possibility that the United States would be going to war seemed remote at the time.

Now, in a bleak desert wasteland, he was getting ready to do a job he hoped he'd never have to do.

For several months after arriving in Saudi Arabia, Nichols and Dennis shuttled with their units between rear area bases and forward camps on the Kuwaiti border. The routine was usually thirty days in the field and three days of rest in the rear. During their shift in the desert, they practiced attack maneuvers, learned how to use antibiotics that would be used to counter a chemical attack, and acclimated themselves to the harsh environment.

"The training was unbelievable," Dennis said. "We were trained to do this exercise called 'hitting and rolling.' It's a tactic where you run several hundred yards wearing a gas mask and a rubber chemical suit, hitting and rolling. It's 130 degrees out. I carried an M-249, an automatic assault weapon, and I worked with a four-man team, providing cover fire while they maneuvered.

"There were going to be times when we might have to wear a gas mask for a whole week. They were getting us ready."

On top of the strenuous training, the men had to put up with blinding dust storms, snakes, scorpions, bad food, tepid drinking water (every soldier in Saudi Arabia was required to drink eight liters of water daily), and heat rash. Some units in forward positions also were exposed to black, sooty smoke from Kuwaiti oil wells that had been set afire by Iraqi troops.

After a month in the desert, Dennis couldn't wait to get to the rear area for a rest break. There were hot showers where a person could wash off the gritty sand that seemed to get on or in everything. The food was better and there were telephones if a soldier wanted to call home. When it wasn't too hot, somebody would get up a football game. And Dennis was able to get together with Ron Nichols and talk about old times at Boys Town.

Dennis thought about Boys Town a lot.

Born in Augusta, Georgia, Dennis was given up by his mother at an early age. He lived with his grandmother for a while, but spent more time in the streets, sometimes sleeping in an old car, than he did at home. When he was placed in a children's home, Dennis started to run away; fighting, petty theft, and other minor crimes became part of his routine. By the time he was eight, he had been arrested several times and had spent time in several youth homes and juvenile facilities, some of which locked their young charges in rooms that weren't much bigger than a closet.

"I remember when I was little. I used to sit in those cells and I used to say to myself, 'Why, when most kids are out playing, am I sitting here?'"

Eventually, Dennis was placed in a foster home in Augusta. Never having had any parental supervision, he remained defiant and unruly. When the idea of sending him to Boys Town came up, no one believed that the Home would accept him because of his behavior.

But Boys Town did agree to take him. On Aug. 16, 1982, the 12-year-old flew into Omaha and got his first look at a new and different home.

Dennis's first few years at Boys Town were anything but smooth. He didn't like living in the Family Homes, where the Family-Teachers thought they could tell him what to do. He didn't want to believe that they cared about him. Once, when he found out his friends who lived next door didn't like their Family-Teachers, he threw paint all over their house. He got caught and spent the summer scraping paint off the brick walls.

Dennis ran away often, sometimes hitchhiking to downtown Omaha where he would work temporary jobs during the day and sleep in the bus station at night.

Once, after returning to Boys Town from one of his unauthorized trips, Dennis went to Father Peter's residence instead of going home.

"Actually, I was turning myself in," he recalled. "I expected the police to come. I got something totally different. Father said, 'Come on in Ron. How are you doing? Are you hungry?' I remember him giving me an apple and a bologna sandwich."

Instead of sending the 15-year-old boy home, Father Peter told him to go upstairs and get some sleep. Dennis slowly started to see that someone did care. Later, he would look back on the incident as one of the turning points in his life at Boys Town.

The people he eventually became closest to were Dawn and Bruce Hugunin, the Family-Teachers whose house Dennis had vandalized with paint. The Hugunins willingly took Dennis in when the boy's first Family-Teachers left Boys Town, and became his family.

Dennis went on to excel in the Boys Town Choir, become captain of the football team, and get elected Homecoming king. He also worked as a Boys Town tour guide for three years.

In 1988, Dennis graduated from Boys Town High School. Four months later, he joined the Marine Corps.

Every week after that, whether he wrote or not, Dennis got a letter from Father Peter. The letters were like a strong rope that kept him connected to Boys Town.

Dennis was glad that the letters had kept coming after he arrived in Saudi Arabia. Now more than ever, he needed a little piece of home that he could hold onto.

★ The gathering storm ★

In the months after Iraq invaded Kuwait, the United States led efforts to convince Saddam Hussein to withdraw and give up the territory he had seized. Sanctions, including embargoes on necessary resources going into Iraq and oil and oil products that Iraq exported, were imposed by members of the United Nations. The military buildup continued, with Great Britain, France, and other nations sending troops and equipment to Saudi Arabia to join U.S. forces. By mid-October, 340,000 U.S. troops were in the Persian Gulf along with two naval task forces and hundreds of Air Force, Marine, and Navy fighter planes and bombers. Despite continued warnings from President Bush and other world leaders that war was inevitable if Iraqi forces did not leave Kuwait, Hussein refused to budge. Hussein again threatened to attack Saudi Arabia, and launched several Scud missiles at Israel and the Saudi cities of Dhahran and Riyadh. American Patriot anti-missile batteries that had been installed in anticipation of the missile attacks knocked down the Scuds with surprising accuracy. But some of the long-range missiles got through, causing substantial damage and some casualties.

In late December, coalition forces headed by the United States set a January 15 deadline for withdrawal of Iraqi forces from Kuwait.

As Christmas approached, any hope that American forces would be home for the holidays had vanished.

Ron McKamy had been at Camp Scorpion in the desert

since September. Thanksgiving and Christmas had come and gone, and being away from his wife and son, there hadn't been much to celebrate.

One thing the soldiers were happy about was that the weather had cooled off. The temperature still climbed into the 80s during the day but dipped to near freezing in some parts of the desert at night.

Now it was New Year's Eve, 1990, and McKamy and a buddy, a soldier from Puerto Rico, were on guard duty. Earlier, the platoon had feasted on camel, a meat McKamy thought tasted like bad chicken. Someone had even come up with some non-alcoholic beer.

At their guard post, McKamy's buddy decided to teach McKamy a holiday song.

"He and I were up there singing *Feliz Navidad*, . . . just to celebrate New Year's," McKamy recalled. "I think that was one of the best times I can remember up there, when he and I were singing in Spanish."

★ Thunder and lightning ★

As the United States and its coalition partners continued to pour troops and equipment into the Gulf region, the United Nations set a deadline for Hussein to withdraw his forces from Kuwait: noon, January 15, New York time.

The deadline passed with no indication that Hussein would comply. Twenty-four hours later, hundreds of coalition warplanes were headed for their targets in Iraq and Kuwait.

It was cool and mostly clear in the early morning hours of January 16. A few wispy clouds floated across the bright moon and there was little wind.

Six miles from the main air base in Dhahran, Ray Huckeby and some other drivers listened as one jet after another roared into the night sky. It wasn't unusual for planes to land and take off at the base, but now there was no break in the whine of engines.

"They took off at 45- to 50-second intervals. The sound of one would barely be leaving the area and you'd hear another one taking off," Huckeby remembered. "If you got on the base it was like a continuous roar."

Huckeby looked at his watch and checked his gas mask on the floor beside his bed. Many of the troops had learned to sleep in their chemical protection suits, and everyone kept the masks close at hand in case of an enemy missile attack. A lot of people even learned to sleep with a mask on.

Huckeby listened to the planes a little while longer, then went to bed. Tomorrow was going to be a particularly busy day.

Ron McKamy had a front row seat when the air war started the morning of July 17.

From his desert outpost at Camp Scorpion, McKamy and his unit watched as explosions lit up the horizon and the "krump, krump, krump" of 2,000-pound bombs hitting their targets came back to them through the darkness.

McKamy watched and listened to the bombing with feelings of dread and excitement.

"From September to January, we just sat there at the same place doing nothing. In a way, we didn't want the war to start because it could mean death. But in another way, we wanted it to start because the faster it started, the faster it would be over. If it never starts, you never know when it's going to end."

Now, he thought, there was going to be an end, one way or another.

From January 16 to February 25, coalition aircraft flew 3,000 missions a day and dropped 90,000 tons of explosives on Iraqi positions in Kuwait and Iraq. First, bat-shaped Stealth fighters and bombers pounced on Iraqi radar and communication installations, clearing the way for fighter-bombers to hit air bases and supply lines. Laser-guided bombs took out concrete hangars where the Iraqis had stored their planes and conventional bombs left runways cratered and unusable. With the Iraqi air force crippled and its radar systems out of commission, giant B-52s carrying massive bomb loads rained destruction on enemy troops, tanks, and artillery entrenched in the desert.

There were losses. Some coalition pilots were killed. Others who survived being shot down were captured and tortured by the Iraqis.

Meanwhile, the American battleships *Wisconsin* and *Missouri*, and other warships bombarded Iraq from the Persian Gulf with Tomahawk cruise missiles, hitting military targets in Baghdad, cutting off electrical power and water to its residents, and disrupting Hussein's ability to command his front-line troops.

From the beginning, coalition military leaders knew that Iraq would be a formidable foe in a ground war. The Iraqi army had a million men, 5,000 tanks, thousands of artillery pieces. Hussein had built the most modern air force in the region and had extended the range of the powerful Scud missiles. And there was the very real threat of chemical warfare, which Hussein had already used on his own people when they tried to rebel against his dictatorship.

Since invading Kuwait, the Iraqis had fortified positions along the Kuwaiti-Saudi border. The defense line stretched from the Persian Gulf to the southeastern tip of Iraq. All along the front, the Iraqis had built an elaborate system of trenches, tank traps, mine fields, and gun emplacements. The Iraqis wanted to make any attack costly, thus discouraging the United States and its allies from engaging in a prolonged conflict that would result in heavy casualties. Hussein believed that the American people would not support such a war and that pressure on Bush at home would eventually cause the United States to withdraw.

U.S. reconnaissance also indicated that the Iraqis were preparing for an amphibious landing on the Kuwaiti coastline. Hussein and his generals fully expected an invasion from the sea.

U.S. Gen. Norman Schwartzkopf, chief strategist for the

coalition forces, had all this to deal with as he formulated his battle plan for turning Operation Desert Shield into Operation Desert Storm. Schwartzkopf respected the Iraqi army, especially its elite troops, the Republican Guard. He knew that a frontal assault into the teeth of the enemy's defense would be costly and would allow the Iraqis to control the battlefield.

But Schwartzkopf did not respect Saddam Hussein, especially his abilities as a military strategist. Even before the air war began, Schwartzkopf was devising a plan of attack that would target Hussein's overconfidence in his army and the weak spots in Iraq's defenses.

The plan called for ground troops and armor to attack directly across the Kuwaiti-Saudi border, just where Hussein expected. At the same time, however, mechanized forces that had positioned themselves along the Iraqi-Saudi border, past the end of the enemy's defense line, would drive deep into Iraq. Racing through this lightly defended area, they would seize main highways and establish supply bases, then turn east. That would put them behind the Iraqi armies and seal off all escape routes.

Meanwhile, two divisions of Marines would practice amphibious landings on the Saudi coastline. The media would be allowed to cover the practices so that Iraqi television was sure to pick up the broadcasts. Shortly before the ground war started, the Marines would board ships and sail into the Persian Gulf as if preparing for a landing. The *Wisconsin* and the *Missouri* also pounded Iraqi bunkers on the Kuwaiti coastline, providing further "proof" that an invasion from the sea was coming. It was a perfect feint, designed to keep the Iraqi forces concentrated along the Kuwaiti coastline looking to the sea.

In addition to the forces attacking from the south and making the "end run" to get behind the Iraqis, two divisions of Marines would infiltrate into Kuwait just before the main attack, then sweep across the desert toward the Kuwaiti capital, Kuwait City. Code-named "Task Force Ripper," the Marines would have to breech enemy mine fields, knock out gun emplacements, and wipe out troops and tanks entrenched in the sand. Heavy fighting was expected and there would be casualties.

Ron Nichols and Ron Dennis, the old Boys Town roommates, would be part of Task Force Ripper.

★ Writing home ★

With the air war in full swing, preparations for the ground war speeded up. Training continued, now with a new purpose and intensity, and everyone began to focus on the task at hand. With the realization that they could be in combat any day, many Boys Town alumni penned letters to Father Peter. They asked for prayers and support. They also asked for the courage to do their jobs honorably, however brutal they may be.

> Dear Boys Town,
> The fighting has begun here in Saudi Arabia and throughout the Middle East. It is January 23. We have not received the order for our first combat mission in Kuwait. I am now a machine-gunner for the duration of the war. Ron Nichols's unit was hit by heavy Iraqi artillery the other night. I believe some of the Marines were engaged in a pretty bad firefight. Two Marines were killed and two were captured by Iraqi soldiers. There were six Iraqi soldiers captured.
> In a few days, I will be headed to an assembly area on the Kuwaiti border. From there we will do night attacks on Iraqi soldiers.
> I will be working in conjunction with "Task Force Ripper." Our primary mission will be to rip through the Iraqi defense by taking out front line Iraqi soldiers to open up their defensive positions. My job will be to destroy everything, something I've never hoped to

happen. I will have to fight until I'm dead or too disabled to fight. Pray for me. I now treat every day like it's my last now. Every night we're dodging Scud missiles and breaching mine fields all day.

Please pray for the Marines, soldiers, and naval personnel out on those battleships who were at Boys Town.

P.S. Lesson: I thought it was tough at Boys Town. Someone else has it much worse. Unfortunately, I'm 47 miles from Kuwait.

Love,
Ron Dennis

Jan. 31, 1991
Dear Father Peter,

Father Peter, I'm scared! I know you're a busy man, but I hope you have a couple of minutes to spare. I wanna tell you my fears, because I don't want my wife to worry about me any more than she does already. Do you know what I mean? I'm not going to lie to you. I'm scared of dying! And most of all of leaving my loving wife and son by them- selves. Father Peter, I need you to promise me a couple of things please. If something should happen to me, I'd like you to be the one to do my funeral. One more thing — could you every now and then check on my wife and son for me? My mind would be more at ease if I knew these things were taken care of.

I've set myself good with God as well as I can. I believe He'll watch over me, but if it's time for me, then he will watch over my fami- ly, too.

I don't ever want to be looked at as a hero, just a man who did his job and loved his family very much.

God Bless You,
Ron McKamy

12 Feb. 1991
Dear Father Peter,

I wanted to get a letter written to you
while I had some free time. We have been
busy and busier each day as the air phase of
the war continues and the date for ground
troops to enter the war gradually approaches.

We have had our daily briefings and listened to the news along with most of the
world. I am very confident in my unit's ability to deliver accurate artillery fire. The lives
of many infantrymen are in our hands and I
know they want to go home just as we do,
very badly. There isn't room for error and I
pray that we make none.

I wanted to write to you and thank you
for the support and concern that you have
shown toward me. I still have letters that you
wrote to me at Boys Town and the ones you
have written the past 3 1/2 years during my
career as a Marine. They mean a lot to me
and always will.

I have to go for now and stand my
guard duty. But in closing please pray for one
another there at Boys Town and please say a
prayer for us guys and gals over here in
Saudi.

Eternally grateful,
Steven T. Davis

February 5, 1991
Dear Father Peter,

We made three shore raids with our
mighty guns firing all night and all day. Been
four to five miles off the shoreline in line to
be shot at by Silkworm missiles. We were
called off the line so the Wisconsin could
shoot some, but then we were called back on
the line after 12 hours off the line.

I miss all of you and I think of Boys

Town. I miss my Family-Teachers. Can you personally say "Hi" to them? They are Chuck and Debbie Hannan and their two little kids Jason and Julie. I love them with all my heart!

I Love You Boys Town!!
Michael Anthony Killila
(Aboard the U.S.S. Missouri)

★ The storm breaks ★

On the morning of February 24, hundreds of thousands of coalition troops, 3,000 tanks, and thousands of other vehicles jumped off from their staging areas to begin the liberation of Kuwait.

Ron Dennis had already been in Kuwait for 72 hours. His unit and others like it had infiltrated across the border under the cover of darkness to start the dangerous job of breaching the enemy's defenses. This meant locating minefields and anti-tank barriers and clearing paths for the armor and infantry to race through. Working in four-man teams, the Marines had marked lanes of attack with red flags, then dug foxholes to hide in until the actual attack began.

With the invasion underway, the Marine units now were moving forward, scouting for enemy positions and calling in artillery and air strikes. The heavy bombing had done its job, softening the enemy defenses and leaving Iraqi soldiers dazed and disoriented. But there were still plenty of Iraqis who were ready to fight.

"Guns were going everywhere," Dennis recalled. "People were shooting and we were dropping bombs at the same time. There was absolute mass confusion. This is at night and I'm seeing everything. It was happening about a half-mile from me. You can't hear anything but you can see people running."

During their training, the Marines had been told to expect

the worst once the ground war started. Officers had stressed the importance of training by warning that the Iraqis would fight to the death and that their defenses would include pits filled with gasoline and possibly nerve or poison gas.

On one occasion just before the Marines went in, Dennis and three other Marines were standing around, laughing and joking. A sergeant had come up to them and told them that the odds were that one of them would not come back from the fighting alive.

The laughter had stopped immediately.

Now, looking out at a smoke-covered battlefield where enemy vehicles burned amid the crisscrossing red and blue tracer fire, adrenaline replaced the fear the soldiers had felt earlier. When someone started shooting at Dennis's unit, he was ready to fight back.

"When people started shooting, I listened, got on line with everybody else, set up my machine gun and let that bad boy rattle," Dennis said. "I didn't have a worry in the world. The only thing I worried about was letting it rattle too much because I'd run out of ammo.

"I never went into it with the mentality that I was killing somebody. When you're pulling the trigger, you're not thinking, 'Oh, I'm killing somebody.' It's almost like playing cops and robbers, but for real. I was doing it with bullets."

In the confusion of the battles and skirmishes, the Marines also encountered an unexpected danger — gunfire from their own forces.

"When we went up, we got fired on by our own people. They don't say much about this, but we got shot at with .50-caliber machine guns that were behind us. It was so dark because of the oil burning that people behind us couldn't tell who we were, whether we were friendly or the enemy."

After one firefight, Dennis surveyed a captured Iraqi position. Two bloated corpses lay on the ground. It looked like the men had been trying to get out of their hole when a bomb came down right on top of them.

Dennis would see many more enemy dead before the war ended. Most had been killed in the bombing and some had lain in the desert for weeks. Strangely, the bodies didn't bother Dennis, even though it was the first time he had seen dead people on a battlefield. To him, they looked like mannequins.

As the Marines rolled on, they captured one enemy position after another. Many had been abandoned or destroyed by artillery or bombing, but the Marines soon realized they had been facing a formidable enemy. They found reinforced bunkers, intricate trench systems, and armories stocked with hundreds of AK-47 assault rifles, ammunition, hand-held missile launchers, and grenades. The Iraqis had been prepared for chemical warfare, too. Many bunkers had a supply of gas masks and drugs for countering nerve gas.

"The Iraqis' trench system was designed perfectly so that when you came up, you had to get over one, then you had to get over another, then another, then a mine field, then a burning oil field," Dennis recalled. "So you were going to get held off for a long time."

Before they left each fortification, enemy weapons were gathered up, and demolition experts blew up the bunkers and other equipment.

In only two days, the coalition juggernaut swept across most of Kuwait. Bombed and shelled for months, down to their last rations, and without any hope of fighting back, most Iraqi defenders decided to abandon their bunkers and give up. Soon, hundreds of dazed, hungry, sick, and beaten men were straggling across the desert, hoping to find someone who would take them prisoner.

Dennis's company reached Kuwait City on February 28. For all practical purposes, the fighting was over for the weary Marines. After regrouping and resting, the company started back to Saudi Arabia along a highway that had been controlled by the Iraqis. Now Dennis began to see the terrible aftermath of the war. Under a sky blackened with the smoke of hundreds of burning oil wells, the Marines passed mile after mile of burned-out vehicles, abandoned equipment, shattered buildings, and bodies.

"I had never seen anything like this in my life," Dennis said. "I didn't know people could do this to each other."

The next day, a cease-fire was declared. The war was over. Ron Dennis had done his job.

About 4 a.m. on February 26, Ron Nichols and 14 other men climbed into an armored personnel carrier and steeled themselves for battle. A few minutes later, their vehicle was zooming across the desert, part of a massive convoy headed toward the west flank of the Iraqi lines.

It was hot and noisy in the personnel carrier. There wasn't a lot of talking.

"I heard one guy say he was afraid of dying," Nichols remembered. "I never really thought about it like I was going to die. I thought about having everything ready. I knew each guy was going to do what he was supposed to do."

The company soon came upon an orchard where an enemy installation was hidden. The back of the carrier opened up and Nichols and the others hustled out, taking a position on a sand berm above the orchard.

After laying down a covering fire into the trees, Nichols took a patrol into the orchard.

"There was a lot of thick smoke from burning oil fields," Nichols recalled. "We went in ready for anything. We didn't find any Iraqis, but we saw bunkers and trailers that had been demolished by the bombing."

Nichols and his men returned to their vehicle and again headed across the desert. It was getting hotter as they rumbled along and everyone was sweating. Several times, they had to

slow down to avoid getting too far ahead of units that were following them. By the end of the first day, they were halfway to
their objective, and as night fell, the men dug one-man foxholes
in the sand and settled in for a few hours sleep.

The next day, Nichols got his first look at the enemy.

"We started running into Iraqi soldiers who were giving up.
There were about a hundred of them. We searched each man,
took away their weapons, and searched them for documents.
Then we waited until the trucks came to take them away.

"They stunk and most of them had not eaten for awhile. A
couple were in bad shape, and a corpsman gave them morphine
for their wounds."

Not every Iraqi soldier decided to surrender, however.
Nichols's company encountered pockets of enemy troops or
tanks that decided to put up a fight. Nichols fired his machine
gun, then watched as TOW missile launchers took out the
enemy position.

"We never really fired at another human being we could see
in our sights," he recalled. "We could see (enemy) tanks being
blown up and we wondered if the guys were inside or whether
they got out in time."

As the Marines approached Kuwait City, the Iraqi forces
that had held the city were trying to retreat to the north. Tanks,
trucks, transports, and any other vehicle that would run clogged
the main highway as the bedraggled Iraqi soldiers tried to flee the
coalition onslaught. But there was no escape. Coalition bombers
and helicopter gunships swooped in, and in a matter of hours,
turned the highway into a deathtrap. When it was over, hundreds of burning vehicles and bodies littered the would-be escape
route.

When Nichols's company reached the outskirts of Kuwait
City on February 28, residents had already begun their celebration. Kuwaiti and Saudi army forces had entered the city first
amid the jubilation, and the Marines followed. Everywhere, peo-

ple who had been in hiding since the invasion in August were on the streets, firing weapons into the air and hugging and kissing any soldier they could reach. In 48 hours, the Marines had gone from facing their baptism by fire to being hailed as conquering heroes.

"People were out on the highway with Kuwaiti and American flags," Nichols recalled. "They were throwing gifts over the fence to the troops to show their appreciation."

The next day, February 29, Nichols heard that the war was over. The fighting had lasted 100 hours.

Ron McKamy wasn't sure where he was going and he wasn't sure he wanted to know.

Driving his gun crew's big four-by-four truck north across Iraq, McKamy kept waiting for something bad to happen. It had been two days since the coalition attack had begun. McKamy's 155-millimeter howitzer battery had set up in a defensive position whenever the convoy stopped, but hadn't had to fire yet.

McKamy hoped they would never have to fire. He wanted to win the war, but he didn't want to kill anyone. And he wanted to get home safe to his wife and son.

The first orders McKamy's company had received had been heartening. Charlie battery was going to be sent to Dhahran to guard the airport there.

"Then they changed it," McKamy said. "We ended up going back to the 101st Airborne Division."

McKamy didn't know it at the time, but the 101st would be one of the divisions involved in the coalition forces' end run to get behind the Iraqi army in Kuwait.

When the orders came to move out, Charlie battery rolled out across the desert with everyone else.

"I just drove," McKamy recalled. "They really didn't keep us informed. You really don't ask. You just thought it was better that you didn't know, because if you knew you'd get a lot more scared."

As it turned out, McKamy's crew never had to fire its gun. Assigned as a reserve unit in their battery, its orders were to watch for attacking tanks as the other gun crews pounded Iraqi positions in support of ground troops. If an attack came, McKamy's crew would have to take out the tanks before they reached the Americans.

Only once was McKamy's platoon threatened by attack.

"We were on a convoy one time when we almost got attacked," he recalled. "Some helicopters got them before they got to us."

There were other dangers in the desert as well. Once as McKamy was driving along, he heard other soldiers suddenly yell over his truck's radio that the battery was driving through a minefield.

"The battery was almost through it and there was no sense in trying to turn around, so we had to keep going through it," he said. "As soon as we got out of it, I remember my chief telling me to put sandbags on the floor of the truck."

The convoy of vehicles and weapons stopped at night. The men quickly set up their gun, then dug bunkers in the sand that were big enough for four or five people to sleep in. McKamy could hear the guns booming all night. Before they moved out in the morning, they buried the bunkers.

While McKamy's platoon wasn't directly involved in the fighting, other guns from his battery were pounding enemy positions. As his unit moved forward, he could see just how devastating the artillery fire had been, and it became harder and harder to look at the Iraqi dead.

"We drove by blown-up tanks and bunkers," he said. "They made us drive through what we did. I didn't actually fire, but I was part of it. I remember when we drove through it, our battery had a real hard time accepting what we saw. Our battery commander got us together and told us it was our job and what we came in for, and it was us or them."

American officers had warned their troops that the Iraqis were fanatical soldiers who would fight to the death if necessary to stop their enemies. The Iraqis, battle-hardened after their eight-year war with Iran, would use every weapon they had, including poison gas, to defend their land, the officers had said. It had been a frightening description of what American troops would face, and McKamy had tried to prepare himself for the worst.

But seeing the devastation and the hollow-eyed stares of Iraqi soldiers who were surrendering by the hundreds, McKamy began to have hope that the worst was over.

"We saw so many prisoners. A lot of them didn't have shoes. They were starving, and they looked so unhappy. I felt sorry for them. I hated them because they were out to kill us, but then I also felt sorry for them."

McKamy's unit eventually reached Camp Viper, the last base set up on the attack route. As McKamy worked to get their position ready for the night, there was an announcement.

"We were putting barbed wire around our battery and digging," he recalled. "All of a sudden they told us to stop and got us all together and told us we were going home. It was over. Just like that, it was over. We didn't know how to feel. Being there that long, we thought maybe it was a joke. Then there was cheering."

It would be several weeks before McKamy got his official orders to return to the United States. But standing in the Iraqi desert that day, shaking hands and hugging his comrades, McKamy figured he could wait a little longer.

On the morning of February 26, transport trucks from the 172nd Transportation Company left their base in Saudi Arabia and headed north with a load of water for front line troops.

Ray Huckeby had been on dozens of missions just like this one since arriving in the Middle East nearly four months earlier.

But this was no routine water run. Huckeby was now supplying a massive fighting force that was racing across the desert, smashing the enemy's defenses and cutting deep into Iraq. His convoy's destination was Log Base Romeo, a coalition supply base located 100 miles inside Iraq.

As Huckeby steered his truck down a narrow dusty highway that had been in enemy hands a few days earlier, he got his first look at how devastating the air war had been.

"We saw one place that we figured was at a junction of three roads," Huckeby said. "It probably was a service station. By the time we got there, it was nothing but rubble and blackened ruins."

After 18 hours on the road, Huckeby finally reached Log Base Romeo. After unloading their vital supply of water for the front line troops, the weary drivers grabbed a few hours of sleep. As they prepared for the return trip, they were ordered to take along some passengers — Iraqi prisoners of war.

"They were anxious to go with us," Huckeby said. "We transported more than 1,500. We brought them out of Iraq on flatbed trailers with the side boards up. We didn't use handcuffs, chains, or bars. You have to consider their mental state. They were living underground for about 25 days, listening to bombs go 24 hours a day. We dropped more bombs in that period than we did during the entire Vietnam War."

Eventually, Huckeby's company rolled into Kuwait City, following the victorious American and coalition forces that had routed the Iraqi defenders there. It was there that Huckeby and the others learned that Iraq had agreed to a cease-fire.

"We left in the middle of a big celebration," Huckeby recalled. "People were shooting guns into the air."

Before leaving for their home base in Saudi Arabia, he and some other members of his company carried out one more assignment — they drove a water truck to the American embassy and refilled the swimming pool.

All across the front, Boys Town alumni had been part of the fighting or were supporting troops who were. When it was apparent that the war was ending, many shared their experiences and feelings in letters to Boys Town.

March 1, 1991
Dear Students,
    As you know by now we have a cease-fire in effect. I sincerely hope that this is the end of the war. Yesterday I flew a helicopter into Iraq to deliver some equipment; when I flew back, we had Iraqi POWs that were wounded. As I watched them, I felt sad. They were just soldiers in the service of their country same as I. Their leaders might be wrong but the men were just doing their duty. They must have family and friends the same as I that love and missed them, too. If you can find it in your hearts, pray for them also.
                        Sincerely,
                  William M. Smith

6 March 91
Dear Father Peter,
    I sit here in the desert of Iraq thinking about how many times I can be thankful for the changes and hope that Boys Town gave me.
    Being a first sergeant in a Patriot (missile) unit is one of the most rewarding experiences I have had. I sit with my soldiers and tell them about a 19-year-old fresh out of high school who went to Vietnam, about the same soldier who at 42 years old, with 18 years in the service, was in Panama a year ago, and now in Saudi Arabia, still passing on those same feelings, only to another operation. Being not only their first sergeant but

also the only combat veteran in the unit
makes me feel good.

> God Bless and Peace Be With You,
> John Browers

7 March 91
Father Peter,

Right now the morale of all of us is really high! I'll admit when I first started in this
war, I was a little scared and unsure. It was
sort of like the first day I saw Boys Town. I
was scared of how it would turn out, and of
the challenges that would face me. But Father
Peter, you know what? After seeing all of the
people, Iraqis included, freed from Saddam
Hussein's rule, I'm glad to say I was a part of
that! I'll admit I was scared that I might die
and not see my loved ones again. But to see
the look on the faces of the Saudi Arabians
who got captured when they returned to their
families! I'm not afraid to say it made me feel
like crying. It is a sight that I will never be
able to describe or forget.

> God be with you,
> Rich Blackwell

In late February, one of the last of the 81 Scud missiles Iraq
fired during the war struck the barracks of a Pennsylvania army
unit in Dhahran. Twenty-eight American soldiers were killed
and dozens were wounded.

The barracks that were destroyed were in a compound that
had been considered for use by Ray and Mack Huckeby's transportation company. It had been ruled out because the big transport trucks would not have been able to turn around in the compound.

In all, 293 American servicemen and servicewomen died in
the Persian Gulf War. Nearly 500 were wounded. None of the
dead or wounded were former Boys Town residents.

★ Coming home ★

Not since World War II had America thrown a homecoming celebration like the one that greeted veterans of the Persian Gulf. In big cities and small towns, parades, bands, speeches, and exuberant crowds welcomed home the men and women who had served. Yellow ribbons festooned everything, a symbol of the nation waiting for its soldiers to come home.

For Ray Huckeby, Ron Nichols, Ron Dennis, and Ron McKamy, coming home safe was all that mattered.

At Fort Riley, Kansas, Ray and his brother Mack were greeted with the hugs and kisses of family members when they got back on June 1, 1991. The war had been over for nearly three months, but the brothers had stayed behind in Saudi Arabia to supervise the transport of their company's equipment.

"You come back and you have to wind down; try to become a normal person again," Ray would say later. "Being away made me appreciate the things we have and things we take for granted."

Ron Nichols and Ron Dennis returned to Twenty-Nine Palms in early April. There was a big homecoming celebration at the base as the Marines honored those who again had brought honor to the Corps.

On April 11, after several delays, Ron McKamy flew into Fort Campbell, Kentucky, to be reunited with his wife and son.

"There were so many soldiers and families there, but we felt like we were in our own little world," McKamy recalled. "I remember when I saw her, she started crying and I started crying. My son was just looking up at us. That was the happiest time of our lives."

In the months that followed the war's end, a number of veterans returned to Boys Town to see old friends and to thank the "pen pals" who had written to them when they were overseas.

As they returned, the name tags that had been hung on the Christmas tree in Dowd Chapel came off one by one.

Ron McKamy came back for his sister's graduation from Boys Town High School in May 1991. In front of the graduates and family members in the audience, Father Peter had McKamy stand and introduce himself as a former Boys Town resident and a Persian Gulf War veteran.

"I remember him saying thanks, in front of everybody, to me," McKamy said. "Everybody clapped and I was embarrassed, but I felt wanted."

Ron Nichols came back in 1992 after completing his four years in the Marine Corps. He visited the home where he and Ron Dennis had been roommates and saw some of his old Family-Teachers.

Ron Dennis's homecoming came on a rainy spring day in 1991. Dressed in his desert fatigues, Dennis toured the campus with Father Peter, welcoming five new residents during a lunchtime ceremony and speaking to students at the middle school. Everywhere he went, there were hugs and handshakes from students and staff members.

Then it was time for Dennis to speak to an assembly in the Boys Town Music Hall. Standing on the stage in front of a huge blue banner with the words, "Welcome Home Ron," Dennis told how he had first come to Boys Town as a scared 12-year-old looking for a real family, and how he had found one there. As he spoke, his thoughts went back to a letter he had received during the war. It had come from a little boy at Boys Town.

"He wrote a letter that said, 'Dear Father, Dear God, Be with Ron Dennis wherever he may be. Be with him,' Dennis said later. "Out of all the letters I got, that one hit me the most. I didn't know how to thank him. When I was giving that speech, there was more to it than just giving the speech. I was really thanking those kids."

After all, they were family.

★ Epilogue ★

In spring 1993, six months after his discharge from the Marine Corps, Ron Dennis sent the following letter to Father Peter.

Dear Father,

The war has been over for nearly two years and now the Congress has just begun to issue awards. Among the awards was the Kuwaiti Liberation Medal, given by the King of Saudi Arabia only to those who entered the battlefield. (It's) made of gold and silver.

Thanks to Boys Town I was saved from a lot of fear and loneliness. I will always be thankful for the many letters, boxes, cards, telephone conversations, etc., from students, teachers, staff administrators, and alumni. Somehow Boys Town seemed to come through again just as it did when I was a young boy, this time in a combat zone.

So it should not be of any surprise to you that I would want to share with you an award that we earned together, an award of hard work, an award of fear and not knowing what's going to happen, a feeling that most of us Boys Town brothers and sisters have experienced. This is something that wasn't earned alone. The Boys Town family was with us one hundred percent of the way; I carried letters from Wegner School students even through the mine fields. This is only a minute token of thanks for your 10 years of support and I dedicate this to the students, especially the youngsters in the grade school, not for recognition but in the hope that maybe this can hang somewhere to serve as a tool of hope for the boy or girl who is lonely and desperate for knowing what's going to happen next, to serve as an assurance that Boys Town is really a wonderful place.

Sincerely,
Ron Dennis

★   ★   ★

Dedication of the Boys Town Alumni Armed Services Memorial

The following speech was given by Father Val J. Peter, Boys Town's executive director, at the dedication of the Armed Services Memorial on the Boys Town Home Campus in July 1991.

Father E. J. Flanagan, the founder of Boys Town, was an immigrant. Like so many others who came from far-off shores to become American citizens, he dearly loved the country that adopted him. He was very proud to see his boys learn the principles of democracy taught at Boys Town and pay back — yes, pay back — by serving their country in the armed forces.

It is easy to love one's country after a short victorious war in the Persian Gulf with few casualties.

The graduates of Boys Town loved our country when it was tough to do so.

They fought year after year in World War II, when so many gave their lives, as well. They fought in a war in Korea that was half as popular and twice as confusing politically. And they fought in a war in Vietnam that divided this nation more than anything else in this century, a war characterized by moral ambiguity and political confusion. Homecoming was a lonely, even alienating, experience. Yes, Father Flanagan's boys have loved

227

this country when it was tough to do so. They have also fought in the Persian Gulf because their country called them to. And they were prepared to make the same sacrifices, even unto life itself.

Yes, our boys have loved their country, even when it was tough to do so. They have passed the most difficult test of patriotism. Will you love this country when it is not easy to do so? Will you love this country when the price of doing so is so high? And this Armed Services Memorial honors each and every one of them.

This place, the ground we are standing on — right here — is a place to honor the men and women of Boys Town, to inspire the young men and women of today and tomorrow and next year to love their country, even when it is difficult to do so.

This isn't a place to debate our conflicts — that's something we have the whole rest of the world for. This is the place to honor our boys and girls, each and every one of them.

They have passed the test of patriotism. They have paid the price. They love America because of its constant struggle — sometimes successful and sometimes not successful — to make freedom possible.

Father Flanagan never was a soldier. But he was a fighter. He served his country in an eminent way and in a different way by making freedom possible for the homeless children who came to his home.

He did not ask what his country could do for him. He asked what he could do for his country. He taught the citizens of Boys Town not to ask what their country could do for them, but what they could do for their country. He, too, had passed the test of patriotism, and we're proud that his boys and girls would do so in increasing numbers.

Finally, I want to thank the Boys Town National Alumni Association for building this Armed Services Memorial and giving it to the Home. This symbolic gesture of "giving back" to the

Home is mighty impressive. It marks the opening of a new era and a new relationship between alumni and Boys Town. I am hoping that you will increasingly "give back" to the Home for the very simple reason that we are helping increasingly larger and larger numbers of boys and girls each year. And we truly need your help, your financial help and your spiritual help, to give back to the "Home" so that Boys Town may continue the struggle to make freedom possible — freedom from abuse, freedom from neglect, freedom from want and from violence — for the boys and girls of today and tomorrow.

For us, this whole town is a special memorial to a war — started by Father Flanagan — that continues today. It has the horror of every war:

— Our children are dying in this war.
— Families are dying.
— Our nation is imperiled.
— It is a call to arms.
— We, the citizens of Boys Town, are committed to love our country, even when it is difficult to do so.

So, God bless America. God bless Boys Town. And God bless our servicemen and servicewomen.

Boys Town Speech
by Gen. Colin Powell

The following remarks were made by Gen. Colin L. Powell, Chairman of the Joint Chiefs of Staff, to students during his visit to Boys Town on June 1, 1992.

It's a great pleasure to be here, and I appreciate the warm reception. I have wanted to come here for many, many years. I wanted to see the work that was taking place at this very important location. I wanted to see the beautiful memorial you have that commemorates the 2,100 young people from Boys Town who served in the armed forces of the United States and especially the 63 who gave their lives for the cause of freedom.

I am the Chairman of the Joint Chiefs of Staff. Now that's a very impressive title; it means that I am the principal military advisor to the President and to the Secretary of Defense. I give those gentlemen advice on how to use the armed forces of the United States, hopefully to prevent war. But when it is impossible to prevent war, then how to fight a war and to get it over as quickly as possible, with as few losses as possible.

I have a very important and responsible position, and in recent years, people have been asking me, "When you were a young boy growing up in the South Bronx, did you ever dream that one day you would be a four-star general and Chairman of the Joint Chiefs of Staff?" And the answer I give to them is "Yeah. Sure." There I was, eight, nine, 10 years old in the streets of New York City playing stick ball, running from cops, because the way you got a stick ball bat was to steal somebody's broom and cut off the handle. And when those cops chased me through the alleys, I used to say to myself, "I can't wait 'til I grow up and become a four-star general and get away from all this."

Of course, that's not the case at all. No, when I was your age, eight to 18, I didn't have a clue, not a clue, as to what I would be when I grew up. I suspect that most of you today have a better idea of what you're going to do with your life when you grow up than I did then. But as I was growing up, I picked up some things that helped me along the way. So when I became 18 and decided that I wanted to be a soldier and that might be my life's work, these things helped me in what I have been able to achieve over the almost 35 years that I have been in the Army.

The first thing I learned was the importance of getting a good education. I wasn't a great student. I don't want to mislead you. In fact, my family gets embarrassed when I tell young people that I was not a terribly good student. When I was in fourth grade, they put me in a slow learners' class. They said, "There's something wrong with you, so we're going to put you back for awhile, until we can figure out what it is and bring you along." My grades were mediocre in elementary school, junior high, and high school. But somewhere during that process, I picked up a good education and I picked up an understanding that to get ahead in this world you have to be able to read and to write, you have to be able to communicate to people.

And I also understood that above all, I had to stay in school long enough to get a high school diploma. Because I understood that with a high school diploma I was on my way — to college, to the Army, perhaps to be a mechanic. I didn't know. But I knew that if I had that high school diploma I was on my way somewhere. Without it, you are on your way nowhere.

So the first lesson I want to leave with you is the lesson of education. However difficult it may be from time to time, however you may dislike it from time to time, you've got to stick with it, you've got to study, you have got to work as hard as you can in school in order to get as much as you can from your teachers and your fellow students as you learn together.

You are blessed by living in this great country. It is a country full of opportunity, much more opportunity than I had when I was coming along. But these opportunities are only available to those who are prepared, those who have a good education. So I beg of you — now I'm the Chairman, I don't have to beg — I ORDER you, each and every one of you, to get a good education, to get the best education. Don't ever quit school without getting that diploma; you'll regret it for the rest of your life. There's only one thing that can stop you and that's yourself, if you don't put the effort into it that is required. You won't be able to blame anyone else. It's yours if you want it, and I want you to want it with all your heart.

When I was growing up there were also temptations in the streets of New York. We had drugs; we had gangs; we had violence. We had lots of young people who were doing things that we knew were wrong. I was fortunate. I had a strong family; I had help in resisting the temptations that I found. But in the final analysis it wasn't my family alone that kept me from going the wrong way. It is up to each and every one of us to resist the temptations that come along. It is up to each and every one of us to fight against those temptations with the help of our families, and for those of you here at Boys Town, with the help of your Family-Teachers.

And among the most destructive of these temptations now, something that is destroying our country, is the temptation of drugs. I'll give you two reasons why, now, and in the future to never, ever experiment, play with, do drugs, or be around anyone else who does drugs. The two reasons are simple: One, it's bad for you, and two, it's dumb. It leads nowhere. All of the young men on my block in New York City who experimented with drugs never left that block. They either went to jail, died of overdoses, or in some other way destroyed their lives. So remember that — don't ever do drugs. It's bad for you; it's dumb.

I also learned, when I was your age, the importance of respecting people — respecting each other, loving one another, caring for one another. And if you do that, you will find that others will treat you in the same way.

And then I learned to always, always believe in myself — believe that I had my fate in my own hands. I never let what others thought about me become my problem. I am a black man. I was a black kid, but for me I used that blackness as a source of pride, as a source of inspiration. I never let it become my problem. I always made it someone else's problem but not mine.

So, whatever makes you different, whether it's your color or your race or your religion or your family background or a handicap, use it as a source of pride. Use it as a source of strength, as a way of getting ahead in the world. Let no one or nothing hold you back. Always believe in your heart that you can succeed, that you can do anything that you want to do, and then work for it and never stop working for it.

You know, Boys Town is a little bit like the Army. In the Army, we believe in structure and discipline. In the Army, we believe in training and education. In the Army, we don't tolerate drugs or laziness or bad habits. In the Army, we believe in hard work and winning. We believe in always doing what's right. We assume, also in the Army, there is no such thing as a bad boy or a bad girl. We believe in family; we believe in taking care of one another.

There was one story about the Persian Gulf War that came across on television that means so much to me because it tells you what family is all about. Sam Donaldson, a reporter, visited a tank company in the desert about a week before the ground war began, and he talked to some of the soldiers out there in the desert. You could see that they were a little nervous; they knew they were going into battle. One of the soldiers — a young black soldier — looked into the camera, and he said to Mr. Donaldson: "I'm not afraid of the coming battle. I'm not afraid about what might happen to me. I'm not afraid because I'm well trained. I'm not afraid because I know my job. I'm not afraid because I'm going into battle with my family. These fellow soldiers behind me are my family."

And all the soldiers behind him started to go, "Ooh, ah! Ooh, ah!" That's an expression our troops use today. They went into battle as a family.

"He ain't heavy, Father... he's my brother." Be brothers and sisters to each other. Work hard. Believe in the concept of family. Take care of one another, and then you can take care of each other in your community. You can take care of each other in your homes. And we can take care of each other in this great land called America, that we are proud to be part of.

So I want every young person in this room today to know that you should believe in yourself. We believe in you; I believe in you; America believes in you. God bless all of you. Thank you.

★　　★　　★

References

The authors and editors would like to express their sincere gratitude to the many former Boys Town residents who graciously shared their memories and experiences in this book. Without their cooperation, this tribute to those who proudly served in the armed forces could not have been written.

We also would like to thank the Boys Town Hall of History and the Boys Town Records Room for supplying historical records, files, photographs, and copies of the *Boys Town Times* that were used in the production of *Letters from the Front*. Most of the letters that are included in the stories were found in these records.

Finally, we would like to acknowledge the following books and articles. These publications supplied much of the background information about military operations and specific battles that was used in each chapter.

World War II

Chapter One: A Place Called Pearl Harbor

Total War, by Peter Calvocoressi and Ben Wint. Copyright 1972. Published by Pantheon, New York.

At Dawn We Slept: The Untold Story of Pearl Harbor, by Gordon W. Prange in collaboration with Donald M. Goldstein and Katherine V. Dillon. Copyright 1981. Published by McGraw Hill, New York.

Chapter Two: Peril in the South Pacific

Bataan & Beyond: Memories of an American POW, by John Coleman. Copyright 1978. Published by Texas A&M University Press, College Station, TX.

Bataan, Our Last Ditch: The Bataan Campaign 1942, by John W. Whitman. Copyright 1990. Published by Hippocrene Books, New York.

South to Bataan, North to Mudken: The Prison Diary of Brigadier General W.E. Brougher, by William Edward Brougher. Copyright 1971. Published by University of Georgia Press, Athens, GA.

Wake Island Command, by Winfield Scott Cunningham. Copyright 1961. Published by Little Brown, Boston.

Chapter Three: My Daddy's Flag

Invasion Diary, by Richard Tregaskis. Copyright 1944. Published by Random House, New York.

The Italian Campaign, by John Strawson. Copyright 1987. Published by Martin Secker & Warwick Ltd., London.

Circles of Hell, by Eric Morris. Copyright 1993. Published by Crown Publishers, New York.

From Salerno to the Alps 1943-1945, by Lt. Col. Chester G. Stark. Copyright 1948. Published by Infantry Journal Press, Washington, DC.

Total War, by Peter Calvocoressi and Ben Wint. Copyright 1972. Published by Pantheon, New York.

Chapter Four: Just Kat

Uprooted Americans, by Dillon S. Meyer. Copyright 1971. Published by University of Arizona Press, Tuscon, AZ.
And Justice for All, by John Tateishi. Copyright 1984. Published by Random House, New York.
Our House Divided: Seven Japanese American Families in World War II, by Tomi Kaizawa Knaefler. Copyright 1991. Published by University of Hawaii Press, Honolulu, HI.
Unlikely Liberators: The Men of the 100th and 442nd, by Masayo Umezawa Duus. Copyright 1987. Published by the University of Hawaii Press, Honolulu, HI.

Korean War

Chapter Five: Pride of the Corps

The Korean War, by Max Hastings. Copyright 1987. Published by Simon and Schuster, New York.

Chapter Six: Flight of the Orphans

The Boy Who Walked to America, by Howard Singer. In *The Saturday Evening Post*, January 23, 1954.
The Kid from Korea, by Henry P. Chapman. In *Extension Magazine*, March 1964.
Song Yong Cho and the Cardinal, by Sidney Fields. In *The Sign*, January 1964.

Chapter Seven: Above and Beyond the Call

The Korean War, by Max Hastings. Copyright 1987. Published by Simon and Schuster, New York.

Vietnam War

Chapter Eight: A Willingness to Serve
Chapter Nine: Promises to Keep

After Tet: The Bloodiest Year in Vietnam, by Ronald H. Spector.
    Copyright 1993. Published by Macmillan Inc., New York.
Beyond Combat, by James M. Hutchens. Copyright 1968.
    Published by Moody Press, Chicago.

Chapter Ten: Courage in Captivity

Bucher: My Story, by Commander Lloyd M. Bucher (retired).
    Copyright 1970. Published by Doubleday & Company Inc.,
    Garden City, NY.

Persian Gulf War

Chapter Eleven: Desert Victory

Triumph in the Desert, by Peter David (text author), Edited by
    Ray Cave and Pat Ryan. Copyright 1991. Published by
    Random House, New York.
Victory Desert Storm, by Eric Micheletti and Yves Debay.
    Copyright 1991. Published by Windrow & Green Ltd.,
    London.

Index

About the Authors

Terry L. Hyland is a former award-winning newspaper journalist and currently a writer on the staff of the Boys Town Press.

Hugh J. Reilly has been a freelance writer for 20 years and is Director of Donor Services at Boys Town.

Book Credits

Editing:	Barbara Lonnborg
Technical Editing:	David Manley
Cover Design:	Rick Schuster
Page Layout:	Michael Bourg
Research Assistance:	Thomas Lynch
	Ralph Wright
	Betty Oas

Cover Photo

Father Flanagan visited the Sioux Falls Army Airfield in Sioux Falls, South Dakota, on May 31, 1944. Former Boys Town resident Lee O'Hern is seated in the Jeep with Father Flanagan. (*Army Air Force Photograph*)